Finding a Clear Path

"Finding a Clear Path is an eloquent invitation to slow down and pay attention, to the birds and box turtles, to the soil and what it grows. Jim Minick is what I'd call a 'kitchen table activist'—an environmentalist whose ideas took root at home and affect everything along the way."

—Sandra Ballard, editor of *The Appalachian Journal*

"Finding a Clear Path is a fun mix of essay topics, with everything from pieces on food preferences to yellow-jacket stings. I can imagine readers curling up with his book while an early winter storm rages outside, for example, savoring Minick's summer journey through a field full of thistles in pursuit of colorful monarch butterflies drunk with thistle nectar."

—Nancy Bazilchuk, author of *The Longstreet Highroad Guide to the Vermont Mountains*

"Jim Minick is blessed with brevity. Each of his essays meditates on one small thing, yet manages to enhance our understanding of the whole wide world. Readers be warned: seeing the macrocosm in a microcosm is a dangerous subversion of the normal egocentric human perspective, and may cause changes in attitude."

—Chris Bolgiano, author of *The Appalachian Forest*
and *Living in the Appalachian Forest*

"One thousand words would be inadequate to describe *Finding a Clear Path*. Jim Minick is a powerful poet and advocate—and person. This book should be in the entire American thought-system. Hooray for this crucial work!"

—Marilou Awiakta, author of
Selu: Seeking the Corn-Mother's Wisdom

Finding a Clear Path

Jim Minick

Vandalia Press

MORGANTOWN

2005

12 11 10 09 08 07 06 05   9 8 7 6 5 4 3 2 1

ISBN (paperback) 0-937058-97-1 (alk. paper)

Library of Congress Cataloguing-in-Publication Data

Minick, Jim, 1964–

Finding a Clear Path

xvi; 280 p.,   22 cm.

1. Natural history—Appalachian Region. 2. Forest animals—Adaptation—
Appalachian Region. 3. Forest plants—Adaptation—Appalachian Region.
4. Forest ecology—Appalachian Region. 5. Appalachian Region.
6. Agriculture—United States. 6. Agriculture—Economic aspects—United
States. 7. Agriculture—Social aspects—United States. I. Title. II. Minick, Jim.
IN PROCESS

Library of Congress Control Number: 2005920986

Interior Photography: **Stan Rohrer, Jeffery Noble, Anthony Ladd, Ariene Gee,
Chris Schnepf, Jacob Bugeja, Govinda Jakosalem, Rich Cutter**

Cover Photo by Niels Laan

Interior Design by Lisa Bridges

Printed in USA by McNaughton & Gunn

This book was made possible by a generous grant of equipment by the Office of
the Dean of the Eberly College of Arts and Sciences, West Virginia University.

Several essays first appeared in *The Roanoke Times* © 2005. "Groundhogs" first
appeared in *Now and Then: The Appalachian Magazine,* Vol. 12, No. 1, Spring
1995. "Creases" first appeared in *Now and Then: The Appalachian Magazine,*
Vol. 20, No. 2 & 3, Summer/Winter 2003. "Health, Hunger, and Hunting" first
appeared in *YES!* magazine © 2005. "Green Lumber, Green Profits: Sustainable
Forestry in Appalachia" first appeared in *Independent Sawmill and Woodlot
Management* magazine © 2005. "Beyond Organic" was first published in
Prairie Writers Circle © 2005.

For Sarah, who has walked with me along
the paths of this book, and
walks with me still

Finding a Clear Path

Walking

Naming It All

Floating

Flying

Contents

Gathering

Growing

Working Among Trees

Following Myself Home

Appendix

Acknowledgments

A portion of the profits from the sale of this book will be
donated to the Blue Ridge Forest Cooperative, a landowner group working to practice sustainable forestry;
and to the Carolina Farm Stewardship Association, in
honor of Mary Risacher and Tony Equale.

Most of these essays have appeared in previous publications, and to the editors of these magazines and newspapers, I am grateful: *The Roanoke Times* and its "New
River Valley Current" section; *The Blue Ridge Press; The
Floyd Press; Now and Then: The Appalachian Magazine;
Wind* magazine; *YES!* magazine; *Prairie Writers Circle;*
and *Independent Sawmill and Woodlot Management*
magazine, especially Leatha Kendrick, Tim Zink, and
Beth Obenshain, who got me started. Likewise, my col-
leagues at Radford University, especially Rosemary
Guruswamy and Grace Toney Edwards, have been stead-
fast in their support.

Many people supplied information for various essays,
and these too all deserve praise and appreciation, especially John Sutherland, neighbor, strawberry farmer,
humor guru; and Harry and Gail Groot, who are doing
such important work. Clyde Kessler, Bob Sheehy, Mary

Ratliff, Blair Spillman, and Bill Akers always answer my bird questions. Laura Polant has patiently answered wildlife and house construction questions. Melissa Lamb shared some wonderful woodland, and Marty White agreed to go on a hike, not knowing he would save me from getting lost. Maritha Lester has graciously shared her plants and life, answering my innumerable questions on the history of our farm. Steve Holliday has worked to save many turtles at the veterinary school at Virginia Tech. And Joyce Graham shared her pawpaws, even though she doesn't like them.

For information about ginseng, black cohosh, and horseradish, Andy Hankins has shared his expertise and enthusiasm. Richard McDonald, The Bug Man, has been a great supporter and help, especially with insect questions. Doug Pfeiffer also gave of his time to answer many bug questions. I'm indebted to the writing of Wendell Berry, to the work of Richard Nelson and Gary Paul Nabhan for helping me re-see the importance of hunting, and to my brother-in-law, Paul Dowdey, for re-teaching me how. Cliff and Donna Boyd shared their archeology expertise, and Philip McGrady told wonderful morel stories. John and Bonnie Dodson have always helped me articulate issues more clearly, as well as been fine friends.

Mary Risacher and Tony Equale offered invaluable information about Roundup and graciously shared their stories.

Dr. Kamyar Enshayan and Mark Schonbeck both continue to challenge us to think about local food systems. Bud Bennett quietly and constantly helped fill my odd research requests, and Ken Vaughan tackled many monstrous tasks. Jean Beasley graciously spent a morning introducing us to many magnificent sea turtles and the Rehabilitation Center's important work. Melody Cartwright and Nancy Moncrief both helped fill in missing information on beavers. All of my students continue to challenge me to write well, and I am especially indebted to Elizabeth Manning.

For time, support, and inspiration, stays at Hindman Settlement School and the Virginia Center for the Creative Arts were invaluable.

On matters related to forestry, Dennis Anderson and Steve Lindeman repeatedly answered many questions as did Dr. Karl Polson, Lynn Grayson, Dylan Jenkins, Jason Rutledge, Dennis Desmond, Anthony Flacavento, and Michael Best. Curtis Buchanan, Mark Lackey, Tom Brobson, and David Brady are showing the way for the Christmas tree industry; I applaud their courage and willingness to share their knowledge. Glendon Boyd let me glimpse his art of making bowls.

At West Virginia University Press, Pat Conner, Than Saffel, Stacey Elza, Danny Williams, Stephanie Grove, and Sherry McGraw have all helped shaped this book.

Though many people have given me directions in my search for clear paths, any wanderings or errors in fact are solely my own fault.

Many teachers have shaped how I view the world and fashion a sentence, including my family—Glenn, Susan, and Kathryn Minick; and Carl and Jerry Dowdey. They all deserve praise and appreciation.

And none of this would have been possible without Sarah, who walks with me daily as we find a clear path.

Walking

Finding a Clear Path

Walks frame my day. Early every morning, the dogs and I head east where I greet the sun and say a prayer. Lost Bent Creek fills the small valley with the sound of water slipping over rocks. Wrens and cardinals shake their feathers and wake their voices, a cacophony of joy. The birds love the morning, even in the rain. Sometimes I'll catch the screech owl's last wavering call descending from the ridge, his "good night" song to the rousing day.

In the evening, after a day away at a desk and chalk-board, I journey out again, this time on one of the many trails we've cleared on this farm over the last ten years. I might hike the newest trail through hundred-year-old oaks to the remains of Ms. Lefew's chimney, the land of her cornfield now towering in pines. As always, our two mutts gallop ahead, Grover, a poodle/terrier mix, and Grace, a collie/lab. Often they scare up turkeys here in this clear-ing, their wings thumping through the pines, their scratch-ing feet having fluffed the forest floor like a cushion.

Usually on these evening jaunts I walk our lane to check the pond, to look for the pair of wood ducks who raised seven yellow balls of feathers last summer. When I see the male and female flying in through the budding trees, I know spring is near. From the pond, if I'm ambitious, I'll hike the back loop, a quarter-mile circle, or if I'm too tired, the shorter loop, complete with hammock and daffodils. Both trails come out at the blueberry field, the rows of bushes turning color, the bark changing from red to yellow, the buds swelling. It won't be long.

In all this walking, I try to be quiet, attentive to this place. Usually, though, I have to first turn off the voices in my head, especially after a long day at work. Sometimes I'll walk the half mile to the pond before I realize I'm still living in my head and not here where I am. Then I'll sit at the pond a while, trying to mirror its smooth surface.

Today in a foggy mist, the dogs and I wander up the bee hill road. We all three start at the flight of a grouse, the explosion of whirring wings carrying it over the ridge. In the old orchard, Grover and Grace take off after two deer. I see only the white flags of their tails arcing over a split rail fence.

Whistling for the dogs to start for home, I notice that I am surrounded by mist gathering into drops. On the pines, the wild roses, the golden broomsage, the spider webs, on all of it, the water hangs like a giant, dancing necklace of clear jewels. I hold a bending branch close to my face and peer through each drop, discover the pointy pines on the other side, curved and upside down. Microscopic life swims in the sea of this drop, having traveled thousands of miles from river to sky to fall as mist here on this hilltop. The shimmering radiance stops me, opens me to the world as it is, in this moment of beauty.

On my tongue, I gather one of these globes of water and taste its cool sweetness. Then I turn and head home, the dogs leading the way, the path through the world, for this moment, clear.

Creases

Two watersheds have created my life. I have mapped out the valleys and mountains of these singing waters in the folds of my grandmother's quilt and the creases in the palm of my hand. These wrinkles in the landscape, and the waters that created them, carry me home again and again.

I am ten and riding with Grandpa on his Honda, my small body hugging his. He pulls over and tells me that he wants me to find our way home. We have just gone through the village of Mifflin, but I am too young and too far from home to know which way to go. He is firm, despite my protests, because he wants me to learn. He points to the mountains, tells me to use them. I wave my finger down one road, and we take off with me clinging tightly, trying to peer over his shoulder. At each cross-road, he stops and waits for me to decide. Once I point, he drives on, not speaking, just grinning at my confusion. I direct him through the maze of country roads, seeking familiar landmarks besides Three Square Hollow, finding none. I can tell we are heading in the southerly direction of home, yet I can't comprehend where we'll arrive. Finally, I see Potato Point School, an abandoned one-room building where Uncle Wilmer used to teach—I know where I am. We make a last turn, heading toward Newburg and away from the mountain, and I look back at the Hollow one last time. I pinch Grandpa's gut just to make sure he's privy to my discovery; he just chuckles and opens the throttle.

Using mountains and rivers as maps is a family trait I inherited from my father and his parents. "Follow the sun," they advised, as they modeled a way of seeing the world defined, not by a grid of roads, but by the hump of ridges and curve of creeks. If I became lost in the valley, they taught me to look to the mountains, and if in the mountains, follow a stream until I found help. Always, though, directions related to a base, to where I came from, to the three-foot-wide Red Run where we caught crawfish, to the Conodoguinet with its rippling folds we floated, to our hayfields blanketed in snow, to home.

From Newburg, where I grew up in Pennsylvania, Blue Mountain bends to the north and west, and South Mountain, farther away across the valley, works its way to the south and east. The waters of both mountains flow into the Susquehanna River, forty miles away. On the more familiar Blue Mountain, the main landmark is Three Square Hollow, a point where three mountains come together, where springs pour out of rocky banks.

From a distance, the place looks like a V with a mountain behind, like a tongue of river between two rocks. I always know where I am if I can find this hollow.

Another memory: Every Sunday afternoon, my grandparents point their 1969 Buick north toward Three Square Hollow, toting me in the backseat and several empty jugs in the trunk. We want that mountain spring-water. I ride on top of one of Grandma's quilts and trace her stitches, marking our turns on these narrow roads. We drive eight miles of hardtop and another mile on dirt road into the hollow where the road turns sharply up the mountain.

On this particular day, we drive past the springs in the deep part of the hollow and travel up the steep, washboard road. Near the top, we stop at the lookout and view the whole valley. I have been here often, but this time with Grandpa's help I finally see Newburg. He draws a map of the valley on the palm of his hand and then points to different landmarks in the valley below. He also points to a line of trees that snakes through farm-land. "The Conodoguinet," he claims. Though I can't see water, I trust him and scan this line again and again. I imagine the sections I can't see, the pool where my best friend, Joe, and I tipped his canoe, the covered bridge we always glide under, the wood ducks we startle into flight. From the lookout, the creek becomes a capillary, the river a vein, and I see a map of the world in the palm of my grandfather's hand.

Before we leave, I find my hometown one last time. A buzzard flies low over the trees, then rides the current up and over the mountain. We drive back to the springs to fill our jugs and bellies, coming away with water, sweet and cold, dripping from our chins.

Years later, I move away from Three Square Hollow to marry Sarah and buy our hundred-year-old farmhouse in Floyd County, Virginia. Grandma and Grandpa are dead, and as I settle into this new place, my directions become jumbled, a torn map I can't piece together. I slowly learn my way around the back roads, but I still don't know my directions because I don't know the mountains and streams. I hear Grandpa asking me, "Where are you, boy? Get your bearings," but I can't respond.

Finally, after about a month of wandering, I discover Buffalo Mountain, a four-thousand-foot, humpbacked peak, a petrified buffalo grazing on a patchwork of farmland. I pull off the road, search the county map, and discover where I am in relation to the mountain. The map shows that this landmark lies about fifteen miles south, a

direction I thought was north. The map inside my head
folds itself shut, turns itself around 180 degrees, and
opens back up, the accordion creases smoothing out in a
new determination to learn these directions and this
place. In my head, Grandpa just laughs at my confusion.
From this point on, though, when I can find Buffalo
Mountain's hump racing westward, I know where I am.

But when I can't see this mountain, I still get lost, still
don't know the waterways. On a topographical map, I
find our home on Lost Bent Creek. A mile northwest, Lost
Bent empties into Little River. My finger traces the many
curves of the Little River to where it joins the New River,
a larger and even more circuitous river than the Little. I
dig out larger maps to follow the New as it becomes the
Kanawha, the Ohio, the Mississippi, and finally, the Gulf
of Mexico.

The spring of our first year in Floyd County, Sarah
and I hike Buffalo Mountain—up the buffalo's spine.
Our feet stumble over the vertebrae of the rocky mountain as we scale two miles and 1,500 feet to the top of
the eastern side. We follow an old road, an easy grade,
until the last quarter mile when it looks impossibly
steep for even a mule. Sweating, we scramble over rock
to a flat knoll, the top of the buffalo's head. We skirt the

remains of a fire tower, walking gingerly on shale out-
crops surrounded by stunted oak, mountain ash, and
striped maple. In the April afternoon, we wish for heav-
ier jackets and tuck ourselves under a ledge, the wind
chilling our sweaty bodies.

On the western cliff, I crawl out to the edge, hold
tight to the gritty outcrop, and watch a rock disappear
into a thicket hundreds of feet below. The tulip poplars'
new leaves green the lower slopes the same shade as the
lichen by my wrist. Distant ponds become mercury in the
bright light, and a vulture tilts into a northern gust. When
I slide back, shaley flecks of the mountain stick to my
palms, glint in the sun.

A high pressure scours the sky of all clouds, gives us
a sixty-mile view. With help from the sun and a map—
the latter a poor substitute for a grandfather—I look for
landmarks, search for bearings. To the south, I find Pilot
Mountain two hours away in North Carolina, its knob
once used by Indians as they navigated without maps. To
the southwest stands Mount Rogers, the highest peak in
Virginia. Closer in, directly west, Macks Mountain
bulges, the New and Little Rivers rubbing its opposite
flanks. To the north, Brush Mountain ends abruptly
where the New River cuts through, and, closer north,
Will's Ridge rests a mile from our new home.

We spend the rest of the afternoon on Buffalo Mountain, tasting winter still on the north wind and watching the season's last juncos feed for their flight to summer nests in Canada. On our hike home, we flush a turkey that clears the trees and then glides down the mountain's spine. For a moment, I ride on its warm back, float above treetops, sail into the sky, and land in a cove a mile away. It disappears and I'm grounded again, hiking home.

From space, the Susquehanna watershed of my childhood looks like a tree so large its roots reach into the depths of the Atlantic Ocean, its distant limbs trailing out hundreds of miles north into the mountains of New York.

From space, the New River watershed, as it connects on and on to greater rivers, looks like a daisy; the Gulf of Mexico, its bloom; the rivers, its long, curving stem.

We live at its roots.

Walking in the
World of Language

My father taught me to read. Long before I could decipher the black squiggles on a page, he had me reading
the meadow and mountain woods. Often we stopped by
an alfalfa strip where he pointed to the field edge and
started counting deer. When I couldn't see them, I whis-
pered, "Where?" and followed his finger to the brown dots
raising and lowering their heads. After a long while, if I
still couldn't see them, Dad honked the horn and the white
tails, glowing in the dusk, disappeared into the woods.

Dad taught me strategies, to look for movements, patterns, or breaks in patterns. An exclamation mark in the
marsh became a great blue heron; the V on the river, a
swimming muskrat. When I started reading the world on
my own, the white fleck on the grass became a wren's
eggshell, the baby peeping for food above my head. The
shiny spot under a log became the salamander's tail; the
whirling speck in the sky, a red-tail hawk. I read with
fascination and glee.

But my whole family also read in the written world.
Every day Mom and Dad read the newspaper. My older
sister scowled at my interruptions of Nancy Drew.

Magazines and novels spilled from the coffee table, and most winter evenings, I knew I could find someone in the den, face hidden, at that moment consumed by language.

I wanted to read this written language, too. Mom sat with me at the kitchen table, sounding out words. Later Kathy, my sister, helped me write my name. We went to the public library every week, and I checked out as many books as I could carry. In this house of readers, I read ravenously. I still do.

Recently I visited my wife Sarah's first-grade class. Like me thirty years ago, her classroom full of six- and seven-year-olds also wanted to decipher the black squiggles. I asked them what they were reading and then shared one of my favorite books, *Blueberries for Sal*. They "kerplunked" with me as Sal tried to fill her bucket with berries, and laughed when Sal decided she wanted to fill her belly instead. Afterward, I helped them write their own stories. They scribbled in "first-grade writing" tales of bears and blueberries, of big sisters and babies, of every wild thing in this world and in their young lives. I tried to write in "adult writing" the translations of their stories, listening to their small voices and learning to read their words. We shared the afternoon, and I learned again the joy of discovery, the pleasure of walking into this world of language.

Naming It All

Naming What You Love

Red bud, bergamot, red-eyed vireo.

I record the return and reawakening of each species in my notebook, my private welcome back.

Serviceberry, toothwort, Louisiana waterthrush.

These records let me know when to expect each new arrival, when to fill the hummingbird feeder (no later than April 15), when to wait and listen. The pages give me room to rejoice when I see the first osprey on Little River, or when I learn a new plant or bird, as I learned the black-throated green warbler's song ("zee zee zee zoo zee") this year.

Chinquapin, squawroot, scarlet tanager.

Once on a hike, while I tried to name some of the plants and birds, a friend accused me of knowing too much, of letting the names get in the way of the beauty and joy in a flower or birdsong. I quieted and tried her approach. Maybe she was right; maybe my mind's desire prevented deeper appreciation. So, for a month or more, I halted the inner questions and tried a new way.

It didn't work. My curiosity kept filling my head with questions. Why did this plant grow in the marsh and this one in the thicket? Why was the flower of the lady-slipper shaped like a ballooned funnel? I could sit, watch, admire, and enjoy, but I craved even more pleasure.

I need to name what I love.

Mink, oyster mushroom, indigo bunting.

I keep a list of birds, an annual spring tally of what lives with us on this farm; what passes over, like the killdeer; or what stays and nests, like the wood ducks. Interspersed are other birds I see in other places, and soon I hope to add a list of all the flowers and trees on our farm. Next might be the insects, starting with the butterflies, moths, and dragonflies. The more I learn, the more I want to learn.

Naming what I love in my notebook also lets me mourn when an old standby fails to return, like the whip-poorwill did for two years. It did come back last year, but will it again? Will it become another casualty, another of the migratory birds whose populations have declined by half in Virginia in recent years?

Naming what I love also might help protect these threatened species or places. On my daily commute, I often spot kingfishers and herons on Mill Creek. What will happen if that land becomes another housing development? A notebook of lists could become a powerful record, a voice for those who can't speak.

Trout lily, boneset, tree swallow.

Red fox, jewelweed, rose-breasted grosbeak.

Bloodroot, raven, flaming azalea.

Seasons' Dance

I couldn't live any place but here in the mountains of many seasons. I need the constancy of change to keep me alive to the world around and within.

And oh what a world of seasons I dwell in here in the Appalachians. From the wonderful thaw and freeze of spring and fall, to the extremes of summer and winter, life flows constantly, rapidly, gloriously, and musically, like Lost Bent Creek by our house. This dance becomes most focused for us when Sarah and I join the cyclical life of our blueberry field.

In winter, the dance slows and quiets. Our field of berry bushes rests dormant, each life pulled inward, protected. We too pull inward and spend more time reading, petting our dogs, and warming to the woodstove. When a good winter storm intensifies this quiet, the snow muffling every breath, we haul out cross-country skis and glide through the woods on this whiteness that holds our weight.

The whiteness disappears with spring's thaw, and birdsong displaces the snow's quiet, the music abundant in volume and intensity. The colors become more intense, the volume turned up on the blue of bluebird, the yellow of goldfinch, and the brilliant red of scarlet tanager.

Spring finds us in the field, mulching the berry beds, trying to stay ahead of the weeds, or pruning each of the thousand bushes. We kneel to the task, our knees soiled, our minds open to the bush before us, trying to see the best form, the right cut.

That quiet work disappears in summer's frenetic pace. If winter is a slow waltz, summer is a crazed jitterbug. From trees in full leaf and turkey pullets scratching the forest floor, to bushels of green beans and tons—literally—of blueberries, the exuberance of life easily overwhelms. We try to move our feet fast enough to keep up, but often we have to step out of the dance, to sit and simply enjoy.

July for us is especially busy. After months of intensively tending the plants and soil, we finally become surrounded by plump, ripe berries. We open the field to customers and soon hear the steady, soft thump of berries filling buckets. Pickers top their buckets and then often rest under a shade tree, content in having picked enough to freeze for the winter.

Putting up fruit and garden vegetables, for us, fills the end of summer and beginning of fall. We line the root cellar with jars of yellow wax beans, New Haven peaches, and Globe tomatoes. Bushels of potatoes and carrots rest on the earth floor. The freezer overflows with applesauce, broccoli, and all kinds of berries: straw-, rasp-, wine-, and of course, blue-. And in the coolest, driest room of our house, we store onions and winter squash, their ochre skins catching the fading fall sun.

Besides sending us back to school and the root cellar, fall also draws us into the woods, away from the dormant blueberry bushes. We cut and split firewood for the next year, the ricks of locust and oak forming small walls along the lane. Sections of our forest still have ice-storm damage from previous years, so we harvest these bent and broken trees, "rainbow birches," as a neighbor calls them. We bring in wood that's already seasoned from last year's cutting and watch the valley below us color from green to yellow to orange and brown to, finally, the gray of winter. The mountains shed their colors first, before the valley, signaling that the cold will come soon.

Content with where we live in this grand valley, we light the first fire of fall and wait for that good winter storm. The dance of the seasons circles back, giving us all another chance to rest and then join again the slow waltz of winter.

The River of Spring

I wait for the river of spring to return, watching, listening, checking shallow pools and last year's haunts. This watery season always comes washing in with wings and petals covering the earth in brilliant song and color, birds and flowers of gold and white, indigo and scarlet, shaking loose winter's hold on the world.

In February, the red-wing blackbird flies into the nearby wetland to break open the ice on this rolling river; to push back winter; to charge the still-snowy sky with a new song. The male, red shoulders bright on black, surveys the reedy stream, chasing off others, staking his claim on the best territory. Then he sings, the cattail bending under the weight of his "conk-er-ee" song, a melody to attract a mate and make a home.

In the same swamps, the skunk cabbage blooms. It too is the first of its kind to challenge winter's hold. Its spathe, a purple and yellow-splotched cover, breaks through the snow in the marshy lowland. The flower bud inside actually produces heat, holding a constant temperature of seventy degrees. This melts the snow, attracts the pollinators, and speeds development. I'm always surprised to find the spikes poking through the snow, purple islands in a white sea.

The river of spring seeps a little faster in March as the roadsides fill with new life. The dandelion-like coltsfoot covers the gravelly shoulder, its invading army of yellow flowers following every human footstep. Because it crowds out the native bloomers, I try not to like it too much, but the bright dials of sun are hard not to admire.

From the sky, the tree swallows tumble in, flying acrobats in iridescent green flashing in the sun. They roost on a telephone wire, then dance above the pond, dipping to drink and snatching insects. I watch a pair nest in a bluebird house, white-throated heads poking out, chattering and watching me pass by every day.

For all the birds, the pairing and sparring begins. The year-round resident cardinals and titmice and the winter migrant juncos and sparrows all feel the old songs rising in their bodies. A flash of red cuts through the blooming yellow bell. Two male cardinals fight over a mate while the snow-quiet juncos test their summer song.

Soon these winter visitors will just disappear. I'll look on the leaf litter where the tiny juncos usually search for food and realize they've headed to Canada and their summer nests. I worry every year, though, about the white-throated sparrow that seems to stay here the longest. His song of "Oh sweet Canada, Canada, Canada" fills our hollow into early May, and though I love hearing it, I wonder if he'll make it home in time. He must, because he always returns in the fall, full of song.

In April and May, the full rush of spring's river releases both the wildflowers and summer songs, especially in the forest. For a week or so in mid-April, I hear a new warbler every morning. The cool woods fill with song as each bird ends its month-long migration through all weather and hazards. My journal catalogs the names of black-and-white warbler, northern parula, Louisiana waterthrush, ovenbird, and blue-gray gnatcatcher. If I look long enough, I find a pair of gnatcatchers building their nest, a lichen-and-cobweb affair they construct before the trees leaf out. Their busy chatter belies their tiny bodies, but not their constant movement. By late April, the scarlet tanager, hooded warbler, and indigo bunting have returned, the bunting hesitant at the bird feeder. Along the river, the osprey perches on a sycamore, white chest on white limb, a fish hawk hunting for a scaly meal.

The rush of April springs forth on the forest floor in bloodroot, spring beauty, cohosh, hepatica, trillium, and columbine, each name as colorful as the bloom. We hike the piney woods, and, like the year before, the pink lady's slippers perform their gentle ballet, a dance with wind and bumblebee.

On our front porch, where the feeder hung last year, the hummingbird hovers, as if to scold me for not having his breakfast ready. This ruby-throated male has flown thousands of miles across the Gulf of Mexico to wait impatiently for me to feed him a little sugar. He zooms by my head, buzzes close to my face, and for a moment, we look eye-to-eye. After he speeds away, the hum of his wings stays in my head.

And in our blueberry field, the bumblebees ride rafts of wind to each tiny, cupped blossom, a thousand buzzes on a million blooms. The field is so full of this river of spring, so full of sweetness, that like the bees, I drink it in with every breath.

Small, Bright Glows of Spring

I hadn't expected a shale barren in the middle of this wild area, nor had I expected that we'd have to climb this cliff a hundred feet above the river to continue on our journey. But most importantly, I hadn't expected to see so many wonderful wildflowers on this high knoll. Delicate, burgundy bleeding hearts, thousands of them, all rooted in nothing but shards of rock.

For months, I had wanted to hike to our friends' house on the other side of Macks Mountain. So finally, early last month, Marty and I started out on a cool blue morning. We walked up a steep incline to come atop a narrow ridge and a clear view. Below us curved Little River, and far to the north we could see several mountains, including the gap in Brush Mountain where the New River cuts through. The water sparkling below us would eventually pass through that gap thirty miles away.

We stumbled along this rocky ridge, accompanied by chickadees and nuthatches, then entered what old-timers call "laurel hells." To travel through the rhododendron thickets, we had to crouch like deer and dive. We both agreed that our wives wouldn't enjoy this part, and neither, really, did we. Our path kept descending until finally we heard and then saw water—a tumbling affair of clear pools, skinny shoots, and beaver stumps—that emptied into Little River. Fifty steps took us to the river where we rested, ate an apple, and took in the Virginia bluebells on the river bank, the small, dangling bells-for-blossoms bathed in quiet except for the bees.

Marty knew better than I where we were, where we were headed, what we needed to cross—this cliff of slippery shale towering over us. "Let's go," he nudged. I just followed along, hoping for solid footing and handholds, and glad we traveled too early in the year for copperheads. We scrambled on all fours, creating footings on a crumbling cake of mountain. Once I slid several feet, stopped by a pine sapling. Near the top, caught in a patch of greenbrier and perched on a ledge, my friend looked over to me and asked, "Do you think our wives would find out if we turned around and drove home?" We pushed on, waded through the briers, crept around the ledge, holding onto a few scrub pines, and then landed on top, staring down at the glistening river below, and sitting beside a patch of wild bleeding heart. This view, both beside us and afar, was definitely worth the climb.

We traversed no more cliffs on the rest of the hike but found plenty of wildflowers. On a sunny, wooded slope near the river, we waded through a patch of wild white anemone, bloodroot, and mayapple, and an early season vireo sang us along. We left Little River and followed a beautiful feeder stream, Laurel Creek, spotting fish darting under roots and a pair of wood ducks on the way. Above this creek, on a bank shaded by hemlock, Marty showed me a huge bed of white and pink trillium, three petals held in a hand of three sepal fingers.

At his home by the fork of Laurel Creek, we shared our hike and flowers with our wives. We even hiked back a mile to a huge boulder where a patch of wild columbine bloomed. These red and yellow cups grew in crevices and bowls, often with little soil, yet thriving on this giant rock. In the clear spring sun, each flower glowed, a candle burning bright.

Drive

The radio is a trap. The tape and CD players, too.

I have to learn this every day I drive to work.

We own two vehicles: a Nissan pickup with a radio and cassette player, and a VW without. Before the Nissan, we owned a Ford pickup, a big, white, rusty hulk once owned by a moonshiner. The radio in it worked for a year and then just quit, no matter how hard we pounded the dash.

When we bought the Volkswagen, the dealer assumed we'd fill the black hole in the dashboard with some fancy stereo. We never did for many reasons—too many choices, too busy, too broke. Eventually, as I made the half-hour commute to and from work, I grew dependent on the quiet solitude.

I learned to drive more slowly, so I could watch the mountains slip from season to season, see the snow melt across each slope to cover only the curving lines of deer paths. I witnessed the sun baptize the river in coppers and blues, whites and magentas, colors more brilliant than the sky's. I came to depend on the daily sightings of great blue herons and kingfishers, and, for the first time, I saw hooded and common mergansers. I still buzzed too fast by these beauties, even at forty miles an hour, but at least I watched the world a little more closely than before.

While my radio-less car released me to explore the world outside the window, it also forced me inward. Sometimes I worked out the day's lesson plan while I drove in and the day's frustrations coming home. Other times I sang silly camp songs or ballads my neighbors taught me. But usually I just followed my thoughts, wandering the paths of poetry and solitude, stumbling onto lines I never knew before, stopping the car to jot them down.

For nine years I rode radio-less, traveled the visual lines of the mountains and the internal streams of my thoughts. Then we sold the old pickup and bought the new. Suddenly I rediscovered old cassettes, NPR, audio-books, and even bird tapes. Every morning and evening the half hour filled with something new—Tom Waits, a bittern's call, and always, the news. My solitude disappeared in the din.

But my world also opened. I never heard the water-pumping, deep-in-the-throat bittern before. On a favorite Tom Waits tune, after hitting rewind thirty times, I finally figured out the lyrics, words I had hummed over for twenty years. And from the news I sometimes heard sources of wonder, like this: "An Iranian toddler, a nomad sixteen months old, wandered away from his family's tent one day while his parents tended the animals. He couldn't be found. Finally, after three days of searching, the family discovered him six miles away, in a bear den, in perfect health. Apparently he had been nursed by the mother bear."

So now, every time I drive the truck, I have to choose between the quiet or the non-quiet—the mountainous world whizzing by my window and whirling inside my head, or the auditory world transported from thousands of miles away through these tiny speakers. Usually the voices on the radio seem too noisy, too full of themselves. But sometimes the voices in my head also seem too noisy, too full of self-important meandering. When both radio and internal airwaves fill with cacophony, when the solitude of quiet only tightens my neck even more, I finally realize that not only are the radio and tape player traps, but so is this machine that propels me down the asphalt. My hands hold the steering wheel, but the vehicle drives me.

Then I stop by the river and get out of the machine. I find a stump and sit and watch the timeless seam of water knit this land, and me, together.

Cruel April

T. S. Eliot began his most famous poem, "April is the cruelest month." I always thought, "How foolish." How could April be cruel when the daffodil jumps out of the ground, the lilac wakes our nose, and the forsythia and redbud color the drab winter woods? How could any month be mean that brings on its winds the hummingbird, the osprey, and the red-eyed vireo? "Eliot, the fool," I muttered.

But one recent April changed my thinking. During the winter when I worked outside in short sleeves, I should have seen the warning signs. But I just putzed in the blueberry field, oblivious to what was happening in the plants around me. The mild winter massaged the plants with its warm winds, coaxing out buds a whole month early, forcing the blueberries, apples, peaches, and all the other fruits and flowers to bloom when last year at the same time the wood lay dormant.

Then cruel April struck with temperatures regularly dipping into the 30s, 20s, and even once into the teens. As the month unfolded, we saw more and more blueberry blooms turn brown, and we heard other fruit growers bemoan the tight-belt season ahead. "Fool" began to apply to me more than Eliot.

Other plants also suffered, especially the non-natives in our yard, like the hosta and monkey grass, both "burned" by the repeated freezes. The hardier yucca and iris just momentarily paused, their tough leaves repelling any frost damage. But one of my favorite flowers, the wild daylily, struggled that year to produce its orange trumpets. The frost turned its lime-green leaves to dead tan.

The cruelty hit me hardest, though, on a morning walk the day after April Fool's. I had pulled my winter coat back out from storage to venture with the dogs, their steaming breath leading the way. Within a quarter mile of our house, they sniffed out, in two different locations, two box turtles frozen stiff. Their reptilian blood had crystallized and burst each vein. Though their shells protected them from predators, these bony boxes weren't thick enough to protect them from a cold, northern high pressure. One had even dug down six inches into the leaf litter.

Over the next year, we found a dozen or more dead turtles, their stinking carcasses testament to weather's trickery, this mean-spirited April Fool's joke.

Longevity

Four times this past summer, I heard the God-awful crack. Four times I jumped out of the truck to see the blood, fragmented shell, and still-moving legs and head. Four times I cried out in anger and frustration, and held the sickness in my stomach. Four times I ran over box turtles.

All four occurred on our farm as I drove slowly; I didn't see these ancient creatures until too late. When I picked them up to bury them, I recognized each turtle, could tell by its markings that I had seen it before in the field or by the house. "How could I do this?" I kept asking myself.

The last incident was the worst. As I backed the truck to park it, I ran over two. We had observed these males over the summer, especially the younger one who had tumors protruding from his neck. We even brought him into the house one time, keeping him in the tub for a few days to try to feed him and fatten him up; I didn't like how light he felt. Stubbornly, he ate little, and every time I picked him up, he stared back at me, his bright, orange eyes saying, "Leave me alone."

I'm guessing he was in his twenties and trying to find his own territory. The older turtle, probably over fifty years old, wanted nothing to do with this intruder, so he was pushing the younger male on to new ground. Then they felt the immense weight of my truck.

I placed both in a cardboard box and hurried them to the nearby vet school where I knew Steve Holliday, a scientist there, who would mercifully kill them and also use them in his research. He's trying to understand the growths that appear on some box turtles' necks. The tumors are masses of keratin, but what causes them? He's guessing it's some environmental stress, like pollution, but like most researchers, he has encountered more questions than answers.

Later that summer, we took a Sunday hike on our farm. By the back property line, near an abandoned log cabin, our dog sniffed out another turtle scrambling under rhododendron. We sat on the hillside to examine its smooth shell, its legs kicking for freedom. Its large size, dull color, and convex bottom shell, or plastron, told us that it was a she. We could also tell by the worn smoothness of her shell that she was very old. When we looked closer, though, she surprised us. Someone, long ago, had carved on her plastron the year "1899."

I wish I could guarantee all of her children the same longevity.

Snake Stories

When we bought our hundred-year-old farmhouse in Floyd County, we collected stories about the place from neighbors and people who had once lived here. Two tales involved blacksnakes. In the 1920s, Dellie Lester, the woman of the house, came out to shake off a rug one afternoon and found a six-foot blacksnake curled around the porch banister. She about fainted, then got the hoe. A few years later, she went into the root cellar to fetch potatoes. In the dark, dank room, she nearly put her hand on another blacksnake resting in a crate full of potatoes. That fellow didn't last long either.

In the ten years we've lived here, we've become acquainted with the local blacksnakes, creating our own snake stories as well, though we've not killed any. One "narrow fellow" used to pop his head out every time we passed the woodshed. We named him Willy and watched him over the years. One time we discovered him methodically cleaning out a stump full of ants, taking an afternoon to dine on the nest. Another time we witnessed him climbing our two-story house to get the phoebe nest. His scaly belly clung to the clapboards while the adult birds attacked, without success.

One spring I was spreading bags of leaves on the garden as mulch, cautiously working my way through the huge pile I had collected the previous fall. In the middle of the pile, I found seven oblong eggs. I called some local snake experts for directions and to confirm that they weren't copperhead eggs (female copperheads don't lay eggs, but instead incubate them inside their bodies). We set up a terrarium inside our house to hatch the eggs. As one veterinarian recommended, we moistened some peat moss, hooked up a heat lamp, and covered the whole with a screen. Sarah moistened the peat regularly, and a month or so later, all seven eggs hatched into four-inch, tongue-flicking reptiles, ready to escape our hands and move out into the world of bugs and mice. We released them back into the garden and around the house, and though we can't identify individuals, I'm sure we see a few of them regularly.

Growing up, I wasn't as kind to snakes. I remember killing an innocent garter snake near the calf pens, and some older boys I knew went to the mountains to catch rattlesnakes. They'd come back with burlap sacks full of writhing venom. I kept my distance but also learned from them not to fear snakes, not to get the hoe every time one parts the meadow grass.

I also learned that snakes, especially black- and garter, are beneficial to the home and garden, patrolling the places we inhabit, eating house mice and dining on garden slugs. Blacksnakes, I've been told, will keep copperheads away, though I don't know if this is true. Like Emily Dickinson, I still have that chilling "zero at the bone" reaction when I encounter a "narrow fellow." Even so, I've learned to watch the critter and let it pass.

Recently, one blacksnake—maybe Willy—slipped into our house, probably following the secret paths of mice. I found it next to the coat closet, frozen, waiting for my movement. I'd wanted to hold one, to catch and feel its one long muscle, so I crept behind it and lunged. I gently pinned his neck between my thumb and forefinger and picked him up. He didn't like it. His four feet of vertebrae and muscle constricted on my forearm, wrapping it in black. I walked outside, held him for a moment, felt again his cool, dry skin, and then released him into the weeds. In a moment, he disappeared.

Later I read about Grace Wiley, a woman who "charmed" snakes, even poisonous ones, in her "Gentling Room." She believed that snakes responded to respect and admiration, as well as gentle strokes and quiet talking. Once a snake calmed to her, she could handle it without fear.

The next time I encounter Willy, I'll have to try to do the same.

Floating

Springs, Strong and Sweet

From moisture on a rock to a trickle into a gravel-bot-
tomed pool, water drips and gathers. It forms a mirror for
all passing creatures to touch with lips and draw from—
the gift, a spring.

Water from the earth often comes quietly. It is an
offering from a world beyond our seeing. Settlers held
onto these life-sustaining gifts, building their homesteads
close by, naming their towns after the sources of their
sustenance: Yellow Sulphur Springs, Cedar Springs,
Spring Grove.

As a child, I rode in the backseat of my grandparents'
Buick when we traveled to Three Square Hollow with a
trunk full of empty jugs. We wanted that cold Blue
Mountain water that tasted better than any well's.
Halfway up the hollow, we parked in a cove of poplars,
the sun dimmed by their tall shade, the wind quieted by
the roar of the cascade. The clear liquid gushed out of
pipes set into the side of the mountain, watery portals
into the underworld. We bent to drink, to capture directly
a sip of this wildness, and came away grinning, bellies
full and chins dripping. Grandpa usually burped in satis-
faction. Then we set to filling the dozen empty milk jugs,

Grandpa filling, me capping, Grandma wiping them dry. The car springs sagged under the load, but we had a week's supply of good drinking.

Years later, my wife and I moved to our hundred-year-old farmhouse, connected to the secret world below by gravity-fed water from another constant and cold spring. Ira and Dellie Lester, the family who created the homestead, found the spring across the valley and up a hollow, over a thousand feet from the house. Ira captured the seep in a springhouse. From there, he piped it across the small valley, under the state road, and to the house.

When the first iron pipe rusted and leaked in the 1940s, the family could not afford to replace it. But they weren't short on time or ingenuity. I have photographs of the father and son working on a stack of pine logs. They felled and limbed trees eight inches in diameter, cut them into four-foot lengths, and bored a hole through the length. They also tapered one end, so each log looked like a long, hollow pencil. The men then tapped these sections together, four feet at a time, to create a new pipeline, a thousand feet in length.

That pipe probably lasted ten years—long enough for the country to find new wealth after the wars, and the family to make enough money to buy stronger pipe. By the time we bought the farm in the 1990s, the spring had seen at least six different conduits take its sweet water to the house. The terrain, the earth, and the freezing weather had destroyed all the previous ones.

The last run of pipe has withstood these destroyers. But when we bought the farm, Ira's springhouse had disappeared. The head of the spring consisted only of a pipe going into a small pool under a few rocks. When a salamander plugged the inlet, we knew the springhead needed work.

We hired a backhoe operator who quickly dug into the bank, shoveling out mud, searching for a seep of water from bedrock. He explained that once he found this seep, he would make a bowl with concrete to capture the water and funnel it into our reservoir. About three feet down, he uncovered the water trickle and also a bowl, already made. Ira Lester, over seventy-five years ago, had chiseled a five-inch-deep pit in the same spot in the same hard rock. We cleaned out the mud and leaves and used it as he intended.

To this day, the spring still flows strong and sweet.

To Pond

To pond is to puddle, to capture, to enclose. The Anglo-Saxon root of the word, *punde*, means "to impound." To pond is to hold water, of course, but also to hold catfish and ruddy ducks, bullfrogs and kingfishers, the floating leaves of fall, the full moon of winter.

Our pond came about by accident. We needed a road to our blueberry field, one that somehow followed or improved an old farm road. This older, rougher track, a horse road, forded a small stream, but the crossing was so steep that the front bumper of our pickup hit the far bank every time, and no car could negotiate the terrain. When the excavator looked at the hollow, he suggested a pond, the dam serving as the road. Years later, we visit this accidental pond every day; it has become in many ways the center of our farm, a point of spiritual calm.

Located a half mile from our house, and in the physical center of the propery, the small pond's quarter-acre size belies its rich life. At twelve feet deep, it has plenty of room for catfish, bass, and bluegill to prowl the depths and then come to the surface to eat bread crumbs in the evening. The bluegills' quick strikes shake the water, while the cats swim like slow freshwater sharks, circling with constant hunger.

At the water's edge, the tadpoles and midges wiggle in the shallows, the dragonflies dancing above. Reeds and sedges line the bank, providing cover for the bass fry and landing posts for the damselflies. On the muddy banks, coons leave nightly prints, evidence of their masked blueberry thievery. Wood ducks dive through this hole of sky in the forest, the splash quick as the hen scoots her trail of youngsters under the cover of rhododendron, the drake circling, watching. Beavers and bats, herons and kingfishers, mergansers and mink frequent this pond, pulled by its gravity; the bats dip and drink, rippling the still water, licking the dew off of dusk.

The pond serves mainly as a refuge for wildlife and for us, but it also gives us food for belly and soul (nothing more relaxing than a slow boat to the other shore). Other landowners build ponds for irrigation, livestock watering, and fire prevention. Ours provides spiritual sustenance. If you have a hankering for a watery refuge, do it right: know your soil and find an excellent excavator. The folks at your local Natural Resources Conservation Service can help determine the soil's structure as well as lay out the dam. Give time to the research of where the pond should go and who should dig it.

Consider your reasons for wanting a pond. If you want wildlife, shallow shores usually mean more cattail and plant growth, which encourages more critters. If you want fish, make your shores steep to avoid the cattails. Tim Matson, in his *Earth Ponds Sourcebook*, offers what sounds like a good compromise: creating a pond with both a shallow wildlife area and a deeper fishing and swimming hole. He suggests pond builders locate the shallow section where the water enters, making it a large area eighteen inches deep or less. This will eventually fill with cattails, muskrats, and all kinds of waterfowl. The other, deeper section should have steep sides to discourage plant growth. For good fish production, Matson recommends ten to twelve feet in depth.

The transition between these two zones should not be gradual, because that creates an ideal space for undesirable weeds. It also allows the nutrient-rich water of the shallows to slide into the deep water, where it robs the fish of needed oxygen. To separate the shallow from the deep, Matson recommends a "speed bump," an "underwater berm" about a foot in height that captures the silt and fertile water and keeps it where it's needed in the shallows. Matson also points out that a pond with these two zones needs to be at least an acre in size.

We already have another pond site picked out. A small stream flows through a wooded hollow, which opens to form a natural bowl. Because the stream falls gradually through this little valley, we'll be able to have a shallow wildlife area at the inlet, and a deeper fishing and swimming hole at the dam, with a "speed bump" between. This pond will hold the wood ducks' "weeping" spring call, the hard tug of the caught catfish, and the sudden shock of that first cold dive into pure, spring-fed, tree-shaded water.

If you would like to learn more about maintaining your own pond, check out the Appendix beginning on page 267.

The Return of the Beaver

Millions of beavers once populated this country, dotting the land with pools that mirrored the Milky Way. An estimated five hundred thousand of these tail-slapping, wood-eating mammals once lived in New York's Adirondack mountains alone. But by 1800 the Adirondack beaver population had been reduced by 99 percent, and by 1895 only five were known to exist in the whole state of New York.

Virginia and the rest of Appalachia fared no better. In 1911, according to Donald Linzey's *Mammals of Virginia*, the last known beaver in the Commonwealth was trapped. No more beaver noses, with nostrils like a dog's, parted the water. No more lodges twenty-five feet in diameter, dark chambers to house families of up to fifteen all winter. No more furry dam-builders to scoop out puddles of water large enough for flocks of wood ducks and geese, their reflections doubling their number. Our ancestors' love of fine fur killed them all.

In 1932 conservationists began reintroducing beavers across our region, and legislators passed laws to protect them. And now, finally, decades later, beavers are beginning to become more common, even a "nuisance," though they will probably never reach their vast former populations.

One of these creatures has been visiting our pond this summer, a regular miniature motorboat and furry chain saw combined. The beaver showed up in April, shy but leaving clipped and debarked twigs at the shore edge. He (we do not know its sex, but for ease call it "he") quickly thinned a bank of saplings, eating the poplar and birch bark and leaves. We put metal guards on four saplings we wanted to save. With his sticks, he built a small, foot-high dam at the pond overflow, and every morning, I tore it out with a hoe. I didn't want the water to crest over and damage the earthen dam and road. Besides, the pond depth was already fourteen feet, deep enough. Mr. Beaver just wanted to stop the flow of water.

Sarah and I finally saw him a week or so after his arrival. Evenings we would sit at the pond edge watching bats. Finally one dusk the water parted and a quiet creature nosed the air, swimming the small circumference of the pond. He floated back and forth in front of us, as if he were pacing, sniffing the wind. When he determined us a threat, he slapped the surface with his tail and dove. We both jumped, then stayed still. He resurfaced and slapped three more times that evening before retreating to the thick rhododendrons at the head of the pond.

Our dogs came with us the next evening and filled the air with barks and racing pants as they circled the pond, chasing the beaver. Though we knew both beaver and dog could inflict damage on the other, we also knew the beaver could dive to safety. Soon Little B, our older dog, slipped into the water and started swimming. She had only swum reluctantly before; now she amazed us with her stamina, swimming for a half hour each night.

Becca, the year-old pup, still feared water, no matter how often we coaxed and carried her in. But a week of circling the pond, becoming more and more frustrated at her inability to chase the beaver, cured her fear. One night when the chase began, this lab/shepherd mix belly flopped and swam, her webbed feet pushing her faster than Little B.

We worried about this nightly event for a while. Were we hurting the beaver? Would our dogs get bitten? But as we watched, we saw that indeed it was a game for all. The dogs loved the chasing, we the watching, and the beaver, it seemed, enjoyed exhausting the dogs. Often he would lead the two, ears alert with concentration, all the way to one end of the pond, then slap and dive. He knew how closely and how fast the dogs swam. And always, after he dove, the canines would bite and choke on the water where he had been, swimming circles looking, looking, waiting for the next resurfacing and chase.

To learn more about beavers, I checked out two books from the library—Hope Ryden's *Lily Pond: Four Years with a Family of Beavers* and Dorothy Richards's *Beaversprite*. Both women spent years with beavers, watching, learning, and documenting this creature's tremendous intelligence, skill, and life history. Ryden studied a wild colony of beavers for four years, observing adults tending their new kits every year, while the yearlings, last year's kits, stayed with the colony to help. Once these yearlings matured, a parent escorted them to other streams and ponds, where they hopefully established themselves. We guessed the beaver visiting our pond was in this situation, probably only two or three years old, looking for a new home and mate.

From Ryden, I learned that beavers mate for life, can gnaw underwater, and stack sticks under a tree in order to climb high above any wire guards. They tail-slap to warn other beavers, to scare off intruders, and just to play. Beavers also do not hibernate, but instead store a cache of food in the muddy bottom that they reach through channels even if the pond is frozen over. Probably the most impressive fact I gathered from

Ryden was the beaver's great ability to keep peace. Imagine spending every long winter in a small, dark space with up to fourteen members of your family crowded with you, sharing food and space. I don't know that we humans could do it, especially without TVs, radios, sunlight, and books. Yet beavers do so without shedding blood, and as Ryden comments, beavers "would have to have evolved a number of complex social strategies, such as the capacity to give and solicit care, . . . to communicate . . . and above all, a high threshold for release of aggressive behavior." Beavers, she found, love to wrestle, and do so all the time, but seldom hurt each other.

In *Beaversprite*, Richards tells her story of living with beavers for thirty years. Wild colonies on her land befriended her, visited her daily, and ate corn and apples while sitting in her lap, the adults weighing up to sixty pounds. To learn more, she captured and tamed two, converting her basement into a pond so she could keep them in her house. She was one of the first humans to have beavers give birth in captivity. Her book is full of fascinating stories and photos, one of Eager, her favorite beaver, sitting at the table, eating lunch with her.

The beaver at our pond disappeared at the end of July. He had toppled two huge trees and injured another, so his leaving was a mixed blessing. He had departed for two weeks earlier in the summer, probably returning to his parents' colony for a visit. But since his second departure, he hasn't returned. Maybe he found our pond too small or lonely. I'm glad to keep my trees, but every day I still look for that smooth-gliding, furry little creature parting the waters.

Sea Turtles

As devoted as we are to learning about our region, Sarah and I also share an intense curiosity about the wider world. One May, we take a much needed vacation, heading to the North Carolina coast and the huge "pond" of the Atlantic Ocean. The mountains disappear in the rearview mirror, and the land flattens to pine forest, and then, after a day of travel, we smell the salt air, squeeze the sand under our feet, and wade in the wide sea, the roaring waves soaking our rolled-up jeans.

But we also come to learn about sea turtles. These magnificent, mysterious creatures often fill my dreams, and I want to learn more than what I can from a book. A book, though, is always a good place to start.

"There are currently eight recognized living species of sea turtles" in the world, five of them "found in the waters of the United States," according to Jeff Ripple in his book *Sea Turtles*. Every one of these eight species is either endangered or threatened with facing extinction, all thanks to humans.

But it doesn't have to be so, and one small group of volunteers is showing how. On Topsail Island in North Carolina, the Karen Beasley Sea Turtle Rescue and

Rehabilitation Center is filled with these amazing creatures and the incredible spirit of the people caring for
them. Recently, while on vacation, we had a chance to
visit the hospital, its nine hundred square feet of floor
space overflowing with huge tubs of turtles, twenty-four
in all.

Jean Beasley, the executive director and founder of
the hospital, rested on a stool to talk with us. A white-
haired, retired teacher with more energy than her years
(and who admits that she'll "always be a teacher"),
Beasley sat among the tubs, and whenever a nearby loggerhead surfaced, she leaned over to say hello to the
huge reptile. They obviously were all well loved.

Every day, each turtle is bathed, its wounds cleaned
and then re-bandaged. Each tank also gets a scrubbing
and a water change. And then there is the feeding:
Beasley estimates they buy four thousand pounds of fish
a year to feed these animals, and a hundred pounds of
squid a week. All food and materials are donated or pur-
chased with donated money, and all of the hard work is
done by volunteers starting at 7:00 a.m. and sometimes
not finishing until 9:00 at night.

Beasley told the history of the hospital and its pro-
grams. In the mid-1990s, she, her daughter, and friends
began a beach-monitoring program to mark and fence off

turtle nests. During this time, they also rescued an injured turtle that they named Lucky. After the veterinarians at North Carolina State University repaired the injury, the vets and volunteers realized they had no place to hold the large loggerhead while it recovered. Thus the idea of a hospital grew. In the eight years since, this all-volunteer organization has rehabilitated and released over a hundred turtles, and Beasley expects to release another twenty this coming year. They try to save every creature that comes through their door, and they lose very few. Though the numbers reveal an incredibly successful program, Beasley doesn't like to focus on statistics. The emphasis instead is on the turtles and their caregivers. "We are blessed," Beasley said as she scanned the room filled with ocean murals, "and the turtles sense that we're all pulling for them."

We paused to admire a nearby green turtle's beautiful shell, each section of the carapace rayed like a brown sunrise. It's hard to imagine a world without this incredible creature, but that could happen. Though sharks and orca whales sometimes eat adult turtles, their potential extinction is almost fully caused by people. Beasley noted that out of the 130 animals the hospital has treated, only two were injured by sharks. The rest were either sick from pollution, cut by recreational-boat propellers, or injured by fishing nets, hooks, and lines. One loggerhead, Swan, admitted in May of 2003, was found floating on the surface *and* injured by a propeller. As Beasley says on the hospital's Web site, "This raises the question of which came first, an illness (from pollution) causing her to float, or the injury."

These are tremendous cuts. Imagine getting your bones chewed up by the whirling blades of a speedboat. Then imagine having saltwater poured into those wounds. A turtle's shell is only a half inch thick, and directly underneath lie its lungs, so it's truly incredible that so many do survive such a traumatic injury. Such injuries could easily be prevented if recreational boaters put a $100 cage over their propellers. They might lose a little speed, but isn't this a small sacrifice?

In addition to rescuing and rehabilitating turtles and protecting their nests on the beach, one of the hospital's missions is to educate, and to this end, the schoolteacher in Beasley shines. She smiles as she speaks of their work with the North Carolina State University College of Veterinary Medicine, and all the education interns and students gain by helping the turtles. But even more impressive is the hospital's work with elementary schools. Like an eager student, Beasley has trouble controlling her excitement at this summer's upcoming releases, where for the first time, a few of the turtles will have satellite transmitters carefully attached to their shells. This will allow students (whatever their age) to monitor the movements of these turtles as they journey thousands of miles.

At the turtle releases, as many as 850 children attend. Each elementary school adopts a turtle and selects a few students to escort it to the ocean. Photos on the Web site show two or three proud "honorary escorts" walking in front of each turtle, carrying a banner with the turtle's name. One of the most memorable is for the huge loggerhead turtle Captain Hook, released in 2003 after recovering from a massive, barbed fishhook he swallowed. The students' banner reads: "Captain Hook-Less."

Beasley likes to tell the story of Honey, another loggerhead, a fifty-pound juvenile swimming beside her in the confines of its small tank. (Loggerheads can live up to a hundred years and reach 350 pounds). A fishing boat captain had called Beasley in the middle of the night, apologizing for waking her, but saying he had an injured turtle. Out on the moonless ocean, he hadn't seen the loggerhead among the fish, so when he opened the net, the turtle fell fifteen feet onto the deck, and the impact literally split it open. Photos show the fractures of the carapace, plastron, and cranial—deep, foot-long breaks down the ridge and underside of its shell. We can only imagine the turtle's pain.

But these are tough animals to kill, and Beasley found the fisherman and turtle waiting for her at the dock. On the phone, she had told him he could just leave the turtle there, since it was a several-hour drive for her to pick it up, but he said that he would keep it company, wait there with it. When she arrived, Beasley thanked the man, knowing he had lost a day's fishing and all the fuel to make a special trip back to the marina. When asked why, he said that his grandson had learned about the turtles in his third-grade classroom that year, and every day he asked his grandfather if he saw any turtles. The man knew he could never look his grandson in the eyes if he hadn't tried to save this turtle.

That happened in September of 2000. Honey is fully recovered, and after four long years of swimming in a small circle, he'll be released this June. It will truly be sweet.

For a great list of resources about sea turtles, visit the Appendix beginning on page 267.

Flying

Nests

With leaves filling the ditches instead of coloring the air, bare winter asks us to look about. Seasons past still offer gifts to those who search.

In the forked branches of a walnut tree, I spot the red-eyed vireo's nest, one I had searched for all summer. Even with his constant "Here-I-am, where-are-you?" song, I couldn't find his mate or their nest, their olive-gray drabness blending in so well. But now, I pull down the branch and see the fine threads of spiderweb holding the twigs, leaves, and lichen together—such a lovely place to be born!

Across the creek, in a tangle of grapevines and rose bushes, I search for the cardinal's nest. I watched the pair fly into the thicket all summer, and I want to see their home. Again, in a fork, I finally spot the cup, molded to the perfect circle of the female's body. Like the wren that regularly builds a nest by our front door, the cardinals used a variety of materials, mainly twigs, grapevine bark, and fine grasses as lining. I even recognize some of our dogs' hair.

Birds use a variety of materials to build their houses. The commonly available twigs, grasses, and rootlets usually form the base, while finer grasses, hair, and feathers form the lining. But birds are ingenious in their craft. Jays are famous for loving shed snake skins and shiny objects, often incorporating foil strips into their dwellings. Large birds of prey and water birds build bulky platforms of branches, woodpeckers excavate cavities in trees, and swallows and phoebes use mud to paste their nests to the sides of houses and barns.

Most of these amazingly diverse structures have several purposes, besides serving as a place to rear young. As Paul Ehrlich, David Dobkin, and Darryl Wheye note in *The Birder's Handbook*, birds utilize a variety of material "to shed water, deter pests, [and] conceal, insulate, and cushion" the eggs and young. The authors also mention that hawks regularly bring certain green leaves to the nest. These leaves emit a natural pesticide that deters parasites.

One nest I collected a few years ago hangs above our front door. Lichen-covered and lashed to a maple twig with spiderweb, this hummingbird nest could easily pass for a walnut. I found it by luck, looking up at the right moment to see the mother hover and then settle on her eggs. I watched her all the rest of that summer, zooming through our open shed or peeking over the nest's edge, her slender bill poking the air. In late fall, when I knew for sure she had left, I set up the stepladder in the back of the pickup, hoisted the pole pruners as high as I could, and just barely was able to cut the twig the nest sat upon. Holding it, I had trouble imagining two tiny lives growing in the space smaller than a quarter.

Perhaps the loveliest nest is the Baltimore oriole's. The basket of woven fibers hangs at the end of a branch too small for most predators to reach. I like to imagine the young, comforted by their parents' song, nestled in that soft bowl. They sway in the wind and feel its power even before they have feathers to fly.

Thoreau too admired birds and their nests, and in *Walden*, he challenged us to be like the birds. "Who knows," he argued, "but if men constructed their dwellings with their own hands, and provided food for themselves and families simply and honestly enough, the poetic faculty would be universally developed, as birds universally sing when they are so engaged?"

What dwellings, what beauty might we create with our own hands? What songs might we sing each spring?

Birding by Car

I don't really recommend this. We already have too many cars on the road full of crazy drivers. But if by chance you too have to commute every day, then consider making that commute more enjoyable by birding from your car. Some tips:

1. Always remember that you are driving. I forgot once and got lost in the black-and-white wings of a pileated woodpecker flapping across the road. My yet-to-be wife grabbed the wheel as we crested a country hill and saved us from going into the opposite bank. We survived, and she still married me, thankfully.

2. Know that your car is a blind, that birds aren't afraid of the huge metal contraption as they fear a walking person. That fear hasn't evolved yet. For example, last week, while driving out of our hollow, we came upon a ruffed grouse. He strutted in the middle of the road, tail feathers fanned out in a dial of orange and rust. We turned the truck off and sat watching him for five minutes, waiting for the female to come compliment this male's display, but she never showed. After a while, our dogs had fogged the whole windshield, so intently

were they watching him. We started the truck, turned the defrost on high, and eased on by him. Having graced our morning, he slipped into the brush.

3. When you bird by car, give yourself extra time. Get off the interstates and drive slowly. Thirty-five miles an hour reveals many more feathered creatures than seventy. My current commute only crosses over the interstate, and on a good portion of the drive, the road parallels Little River, so I'm lucky and always looking. In the winter, especially, with the trees bare, I can see more. Often the white-bubbled head of the hooded merganser will glint across the water, or I'll spy the steely gray back of a great blue heron. Sometimes I'll catch a great blue perched high in a dead tree, its huge slump of a figure warming in the morning sun, slowly waking before the hunt for breakfast. My day seems empty if I don't see at least one heron or kingfisher.

4. Learn the habits and habitats of birds. Along the same stretch of river, every spring, I focus more on the tops of the sycamores than on the surface of the water. I keep looking for a different patch of white, the large breast of the osprey as it migrates through to nesting waters in the north. I usually count six or so every year and always get close enough to one to see its yellow

pupil stare me down. Once I even witnessed one dive and catch a fish, as we both moved along at fifteen miles per hour. But oh how much more gracefully that bird, any bird, can move than we in our four-wheeled machines.

5. Check out telephone lines, birdhouses, or other favorite roosts. I often see kestrels and doves silhouetted against the morning sky, and sometimes meadowlarks will sing from those lines, their brilliant yellow bellies puffed out to mimic the sun.

6. In warm weather, drive with your window down and listen. On annual bird counts, I'm always amazed at friends who can identify some rare warbler just by hearing a snippet of its song. We'll stop and search and finally find the discreet bird hidden in some pawpaws, but not without first hearing the song.

7. Again, remember that you're driving. If you see some outlandishly remarkable bird, pull over. Don't make your spouse grab that steering wheel. Get home safely, and do some better, cleaner, safer birding by going for a walk.

Vanishing Birds

My grandfather got me started. Sunday evenings after Lawrence Welk, he turned on the phonograph and played the Peterson's *Field Guide to Bird Songs* album. Through the scratchy speakers, a man's deep voice would identify the bird, then the creature would call, squawk, whistle, thump, or sing melodiously. All of these wondrous sounds and mysterious names like "whooping crane" and "pied-billed grebe" compelled me to listen closely and follow along in our bird book. I had become a birder and I was only six years old.

The year Grandpa bought the bird album, I saw my first male bluebird near our pond, a bright blue piece of heaven with wings. I followed him to find a nest in a hollow fence post, and inside, three wide mouths greeted my curious eyes. My own hunger had just started.

That's been over thirty years ago, and still I watch birds, especially in the spring when the migrants return from the south. To think, that tiny hummingbird who weighs less than a dime flies across the five-hundred-mile-wide Gulf of Mexico without resting! Yet this bird, and many others, make the long journey from Central or South America to our front porches every year, with no gas-powered engines, no supersonic noise, only wings and a sweet melody.

Though I know I'll encounter many berry-eating birds in our blueberry field, I still welcome them (except maybe the starlings). They all need our help as their numbers steadily drop. Over the decades, ornithologists across the southeast have documented that the population of migratory birds has fallen by at least 50 percent. Many migrants are decreasing by 5 to 10 percent each year. That is too many and too fast.

Why should we care? Granted, birds like the house sparrow and crow can ruin a garden or orchard. But the vast majority of birds greatly benefit us. Some of the most voracious eaters of insects include chickadees, wrens, phoebes, swallows, vireos, and warblers. The pair of Carolina wrens at our place, for example, raises at least three broods of three to five nestlings each year. In the summer, these birds are almost exclusively insect eaters, so imagine how many bugs it takes to raise this many chicks!

Birds also greatly aid trees, and a study done in Missouri not long ago proved this. Researchers covered oak trees with nets that allowed insects to enter but excluded birds. They found over a two-year period that netted trees had twice as many insects and suffered twice as much damage. The loss of these beautiful, industrious songbirds will affect us all.

Since childhood, I've wanted to sate my hunger for avian knowledge, so I've tried to find bird-brained friends. I joined a local bird club that tried to prevent—or at least monitor—the loss in bird population. One Saturday, I participated in my first annual spring migration count for my home county. Volunteers traveled all over the area, counting every bird they heard or saw. We wanted not to take a census (a task beyond the scope of a handful of volunteers), but a snapshot of what birds are actually here. With each successive annual snapshot, we can compare population numbers to those of previous years for a rough estimate of which birds are improving, stabilizing, or losing their numbers.

Some of the highlights from that first count included a rose-breasted grosbeak at my feeder; magnolia, chestnut-sided, and hooded warblers all feasting on bugs; and ten Baltimore orioles dining on tent caterpillars. Together, the teams counted ninety-one species, a decent number for a cold, windy day with snow flurries. Still, I didn't see any thrushes, birds I used to listen to regularly on my grandfather's album.

My grandfather has long since died, but I still have the bird album and listen to it occasionally. Every time the man's deep voice says, "Ivory-billed woodpecker," I listen intently. That bird hadn't been sighted for over sixty years, everyone thinking it extinct. The call that fills my living room no longer blankets the woods. The booming taps that resonate through the stereo speakers from this crow-sized bird only produce a hollow echo, but thankfully, now we know other ivory-bills can answer this lonesome call.

To learn more about songbirds, turn to the Appendix beginning on page 267.

Monarchs: Flying Poetry

Late summer and the thistle thick. My wife and I hike through woods up a steep hill, the heat penetrating like the locusts' song. At the top, the oaks and maples break into a bald, a hole to the sky, an opening to butterflies. We are surrounded by color—green spikes of grass, white and blue of sky, deep pink of thistle bloom, and the orange fire of monarchs—hundreds of monarchs. They've come to this abandoned pasture to dine on thistle nectar.

I grew up chopping thistle, the prickly weed that looks like a miniature artichoke and which cattle hate. Grandma paid me nickels and dimes for every one cut. I took the hoe into the pasture, beyond the reach of her arthritic knees, and sweated with each swing. She watched from the kitchen, praised the "clean" field, and pointed out any I missed. I went back out, questioning her eyesight under my breath, and chopped the stray weeds before she paid me the change.

But here on this knoll years later, the bull and Canadian thistle hold a beauty rich and deep. These royal butterflies, tethered by tongues, dip into each bloom, draw food for their long flight south. "A poem with wings," someone once rightly described these creatures.

I want to hold one, to feel the feet, the flutter of wing, the tongue probing each crevice of my fingerprints. I have held other butterflies, fritillaries and skippers, gently nudging a finger under back legs, slowly waiting for each foot to rest on my hand. But fritillaries are tamer, less cautious than these monarchs. Every butterfly I try to touch flies quickly away. So we sit eye-level to these quiet creatures. We are silenced by their size, their speed, their incredible journey, and always, their immense beauty—a network of veins on a delicate cloth, a black web on an orange sun.

Monarchs not only fascinate with their beauty, but also with their amazing life history. They are one of the few butterflies to migrate south, like birds and whales, to avoid northern winters. But unlike those travelers, a monarch weighs less than a penny. These journeys, especially for butterflies east of the Rockies, can run distances of three thousand miles. The creatures on our high knoll were "fueling up" for such a journey to the warm air of Mexico.

These are not the same monarchs, though, that flew north last spring. Instead they are the great-great-grandchildren of those previous winged creatures. Imagine being able to travel, by your own energy, thousands of miles to the same home where your great-great-grandparents spent the winter holidays. And envision doing this without ever knowing your great-great-grandparents or having seen your destination. Despite years of study, the mystery of how monarchs hone in on path and place eludes human curiosity. We have much yet to learn.

We also still have much to do. As in most of our world, human activity has harmed these flying wonders. In Mexico, where monarchs cluster so thickly in the winter that they sometimes break branches, logging threatens their forests of refuge. According to an article by Pat Durkin published by *National Geographic News*, a tenth of the high mountain forests that existed just thirty years ago remain. Several organizations, like the World Wildlife Fund and Monarch Watch, have attempted to prevent logging in these sanctuaries, while also giving the people who live there other more sustainable incomes. The results have been mixed.

But an even greater threat to the monarchs might exist in the United States and Canada. Here in their breeding ground, herbicides have reduced the number of plants that support them, like milkweed, while insecticides aimed at gypsy moths and other pests have also inadvertently killed monarchs. Likewise, the spread of new houses, malls, and roads often wipes out good butterfly habitat. Even though monarchs currently number in the millions, they will become more threatened with our constant desire for growth.

A week later when we hike back to the hilltop, we find the farmer has mowed all the thistle, and the butterflies have disappeared. Though I continue to harbor my grandmother's and this farmer's strong hatred of thistle, I know a few patches of this weed will always survive on our own farm. Hopefully the butterflies will continue to return.

If you are interested in reading more about the monarch butterfly, see the Appendix beginning on page 267.

Mirrored Intruder

The tufted titmouse has taken over the front window. Every morning around 6:30 or 7:00, he perches on the nearby lilac, sings his three clear whistles, and then lands on the windowsill. He looks in, his black eyes shining, head bobbing from side to side. Then he flutters and taps his beak on the windowpane. He knocks for five minutes or so, only to return and strike again. We can hear his small, hollow pecks throughout the house. He taps like a woodpecker who mistakes a window for a bug-laden tree.

The titmouse replaced his larger tufted neighbor, the cardinal. For the past three years, the male redbird performed this rapping ritual at the same front window. Like the titmouse, he too came early, and if we tried to sleep in on a Saturday, he made enough noise to wake us. Sometimes I would watch him through the old, wavy glass, the brilliant red crown feathers rising with each attack, black eyes glinting. If I waited quietly, I could sit inches away on the other side of the thin pane. He never saw me as he perched on the sill, sang his "cheer cheer cheer" song, and yellow-beaked that glass as hard as he could. I don't know why the cardinal relinquished his pecking spot to the titmouse, but I'm glad they both don't come at the same time. They might break the glass.

"Why all the noise and fuss?" I wondered. Both birds seemed to be normal. They didn't fly sideways or sing backwards, and I didn't see any odd growths on their heads, though I wondered how their beaks could withstand such constant hammering. Why the persistent knocking? I knew they didn't really want me to open the window for them to enter. They had nests of their own nearby.

About a month after the cardinal started his ritual that first year, I had the ladder up to the window so I could wash it. The sun hadn't come around to that side of the house yet, so as I washed away the winter's dust, my reflection became clear. I stopped wiping and just looked at my own reflection. The cardinal, too, was seeing his own image. But really, the cardinal was seeing an intruder, an enemy, another brilliant red male to attack and chase away from his territory. Every time he looked, and in every mirror of a pane, he saw the same enemy.

This past weekend I washed the window again. When I went in for lunch, the titmouse perched on the creeper vine next to the window, his rusty side feathers surrounded by soft gray. He set to tapping, as if he wanted part of my sandwich. But he really just wanted that trespasser to fly away, that intruder he saw in himself.

Terrifying Beauty

Late evening, the light fading, I work in the garden and listen. The sound of two juvenile great horned owls fills the hollow, their squawk a cross between a deer snort and a raven croak. They sit on the next hill, and this squawk is their plea for their parents to come with food.

The first time I heard this two years ago, the ascending squawk had me stumped. What kind of a creature made this racket? The noise came from thick pines behind our house, and try as I might, I couldn't locate the source. I pulled out bird recordings, but nothing matched. So I called my birder friends, imitated the squawk on the phone, and they identified it as an immature great horned owl.

I see the parent owls often, especially in the bare trees of winter. One will perch in a snag across the hollow from our house. The horned ear feathers swivel, the head pauses and turns, and the huge, brown body waits for a mouse's slightest rustle. What chill must his hoot give to mice and rabbits, to all the creatures he pierces with razor-edged talons? Once I walked right under him, surprised by his fearlessness. He peered down, examining our dogs, twisting his head to follow our path. He has dined on skunks and snakes, so I know he could kill and eat our smallest dog. I hurried on, keeping our terrier close.

Usually, though, these night hunters just eat mice. Sometimes under an oak I'll find the owl's pellets, egg-size gray masses of hair and bone. These birds swallow mice whole, then later regurgitate what they can't digest, one pellet per prey. With a stick, I pick apart each pellet, separating the matted hairs to find tiny bones, hips and ribs and skull.

When we lived on a different farm, I marveled at another great horned owl family. I saw them regularly at dusk in the oak forest, the parents hissing and clacking, the young whistling for food. And always in the subconscious ooze of night, I woke and heard their five hoots, the female's quicker than the male's.

We had chickens then, six Rhode Island Reds that came wobbling side-to-side when we called. They ate tomatoes out of our hands and pecked at worms in the just-turned garden. One morning when I went to feed them, I found their bloody bodies strewn across the pen. The owls, or maybe weasels, had come in the night and found an easy meal. One by one, they beheaded and debrained each bird.

They are hunger defined, these owls. Their feathers slice the night more silently than any other bird, and the shape of their faces funnels the infinitesimal sound of mouse movement into their ears, ears like no other creature's. The openings are asymmetrical, one ear slightly back from the other. An owl can precisely pinpoint the mouse's twitch because the sound reaches each ear at a slightly different time–and a heard mouse is usually a dead one.

Eventually these young owls I hear squawking every evening will test their nascent hoots, will learn to listen and glide with deadly accuracy, will call us all out of the night to know that death is full of terrifying beauty.

Counting Birds at Christmas

We sit at the edge of a cornfield where ice glistens on each beaten stalk. Even with layers of sweaters, long johns, and wool mittens, even with the car heater cranked full blast, my friend Mary and I both shiver. As part of the annual Christmas Bird Count, we are trying to identify the number of juncos and sparrows feeding on the ground, but the car windows keep fogging.

Then the car's "Service Engine" warning light begins to flash and beep. "What's that about?" Mary asks.

"I think we're draining too much heat from the engine. It's just too cold."

We quickly tally what birds we can with the windows rolled down, then turn around and head to Hardee's for heat, coffee, and a break. When we pass the bank, we see the temperature hasn't changed in two hours; the sign still reads nine degrees.

Why would twenty or so regular folks gather to count birds on such a bitter morning? Besides being bird-crazy, people join the Christmas Count mainly to get a sense of what species overwinter here. Most birders would also include curiosity and benevolence toward feathered creatures, along with friendship, pleasure, and a respect for tradition. We want to tell old jokes with older friends, but more importantly, we want to share our discoveries of what's come south or staying for the winter. Who but a fellow birder would appreciate the startling sight of a black-and-white speckled loon diving for breakfast, or the tinkling song of the winter wren? We seek beauty.

We're not alone in this. The Audubon Society started the Christmas Bird Count in 1899, and the Blacksburg, Virginia count was initiated in 1934. The idea has spread and continued, with thousands of groups ranging across North, Central, and South America. The count occurs during the same three-week holiday period every year, with each event focused on a fifteen-mile radius.

Because of the wide range of experience and year-to-year differences in the number of counters, each count is highly variable and not terribly scientific. Yet it does give a basic feel for the movement and populations of birds over the years. For example, some years here in the New River Valley, we find huge flocks of evening grosbeaks, waxwings, and horned larks; some years we don't see any.

Bill Akers started counting in his hometown of Radford in 1964; his good friend Blair Spillman joined him three years later. Together, they haven't missed a count in these four intervening decades. They like to explore nature, whatever the weather, to see what's happening in the natural and man-made communities, and they enjoy getting together for a few good laughs. On average, they and the Radford counters see forty to forty-five species, from cardinals and chickadees to mergansers and buffleheads, while the whole New River group averages sixty to seventy bird types. But as Bill comments, "We find pretty much your blue-collar birds; no 'oo-ah' birds here." Sometimes on the river they'll find redhead, ruddy duck, or common goldeneye. Once, a catbird surprised them in a fencerow. The gray mimic was supposed to be in Florida that time of year.

Over the scope of his decades of counting, Bill has watched the effect of suburban sprawl on the birds. "We still find most of the birds, just in less numbers," he says. "Every year their overwintering area becomes a little more compressed." Some birds have returned to this area, like the cormorants. Others have increased in number, like, of course, the Canadian geese. But most are struggling.

Still, Bill and Blair regularly find much to hearten them. Recently, as they approached a grove of trees, they kept hearing a "popcorn" sound. High in the trees, a flock of evening grosbeaks ate poison ivy seeds, their massive bills cracking the dried fruit. At a different haunt, every year the two men round the same bend in a dirt road, wondering if they'll ever see snipes again. And just about every winter, the birds seek this one ditch, their long bills probing the mud for worms.

Homes for the Holidays

At Christmas a few years ago, I totally surprised Sarah with three home-made gifts. This was no small feat considering I'd had to smuggle the materials to Charlotte, where we visited her family at Thanksgiving, build the gifts there in her father's well-equipped workshop, then smuggle them back to Virginia in the trunk of the car. They were big, so Sarah knew something suspicious was hidden there under plastic, and I enjoyed teasing her, trying to make her guess. Every time she guessed wrongly, I just chuckled. She really had no idea.

The gifts: two wood duck houses and a bat house. We had just built a quarter-acre pond, and we wanted to attract more wildlife to it. As the duck flies, we're only one mile from Little River, so we figured the birds would find us. They did. Small flocks of wood ducks came sailing in, and from who-knows-where bats at evening swirled around the open sky above the pond, stirring up the stars.

Any human dwelling near water, or any farm with a pond or stream, should have a wood duck house. These beautiful creatures, once almost destroyed by over-hunting, still shy from human contact. Yet their grace and color deserve nurturing and preserving. We have spent hours secretly watching the male, with his red eyes and white-and-green shining head, courting the female. Later, we've watched the female, with her white eye-ring, lead her flock of young on journeys to the river. Secretive and often undetected, wood ducks have an uncanny ability to quietly fly directly into the small hole of the birdhouse, a sight I've yet to witness despite much time waiting and watching. Their favorite nesting trees, snags full of woodpecker holes, are not plentiful, so con-sider building a box house for these creatures.

Making It Happen

The boxes measure one foot by one foot by two feet with a roof sloping from front to back to drain water. Make the entrance hole a four-inch circle located three inches below the roof, and use rough-cut lumber—the more weather-resistant the better. A small opening can be cut out of the side and covered with a hinged wooden door for ease in future cleaning. Drill five 1/4-inch holes in the bottom for drainage. On the inside of the front panel, sta-ple a four-inch strip of hardware cloth or dent the wood with a hammer claw to give the ducklings good footing for their first journey out of their home. Fill the boxes with four inches of sawdust for good bedding, and locate the houses close to, or even over, water. The most dangerous time in a wood duck's life is when it first jumps from the nest and travels to water. The farther the water, the more treacherous the journey.

Just as every dwelling near water should have a wood duck box, every house, wherever it's located, should have a bat house. These mammals eat up to three thousand bugs a night, which is a boon for any gardener who dislikes grasshoppers, corn borers, or cutworms, or for any backyard picnicker who dislikes mosquitoes. Plus, they are simply fascinating to watch, weaving through the night air, quietly fluttering to and fro, darting acrobatically. Our irrational fear of these creatures, mammals just like us, is unfounded, and has caused dangerous declines in their populations. They, like the wood ducks, need our help.

A bat house looks like a duck house, also measuring one foot by one foot by two feet, but the bat house has no front entrance hole and no floor. These creatures enter, instead, where the floor would be. The inside also is constructed differently. Bats like tight, dark sleeping quarters, so partition the space with additional boards at intervals ranging from three-fourths of an inch to an inch and a half. Before you nail these in place, dent *all* surfaces of the boards with the claw of a hammer, just like with the front side of the duck house. These dents allow the bats to crawl into the box and grip the wood for a good day's sleep, hanging upside down.

Again, choose weather-resistant wood or just use what's on hand, which for us is plentiful pine. Definitely avoid treated lumber, since the chemicals can cause illness. Locate bat houses high, away from the grasp of predators, and if possible, near water and facing east or south, so the sun warms them as they sleep.

Often last summer, we would walk to the pond at dusk to be rewarded by the sight of either the wood ducks or bats. The ducks, in twos and threes, flew in for a night's roost, their wings whistling as they landed. At the same time, the bats woke and tumbled and dove and quietly gobbled up their thousands upon thousands of insects. Occasionally in the dwindling twilight, we saw the silhouette of a bat dipping to the pond for a drink, circles of ripples slowly fading.

For more information on bats, take a look at the Appendix beginning on page 267.

Gathering

Miracle Morels

Last spring, while I worked in the garden, a young man stopped his truck to talk. His first question, "Find any merkles?" startled me, sent me stumbling to understand this word. It sounded like "miracles," and I had seen lots of miracle-new sprouts in the garden, but I couldn't imagine him, a stranger, asking me about heavenly occurrences here on earth. Then I realized: he was asking about morel mushrooms, those miracle merkles that appear in April every year.

I told him I had found "a few," but I wasn't about to give away the location of my favorite patch. We talked about a couple of wild apple trees nearby, ones I had checked once without any luck. I told him he was more than welcome to look there. I didn't tell him that the miracles I harvested secreted themselves on the other side of the farm, under some other ancient apple trees.

Morels, *Morchella angusticeps*, pop up from the beat-up brown of the forest floor in April and May, right as the early wildflowers peak. Their caps have the wrinkled texture of a brain, wave upon wave of brown wiggles atop a cream-colored stem. They like rainy weather and usually grow in patches under certain trees, like poplar, apple, ash, and elm. As with all wild fungi, if you've never gathered, use caution and a good identification book.

Friends studying law in Montana have been harvesting morels in the Rocky Mountains the last two years and making around $2000 a season. They've witnessed more experienced foragers wildcrafting a hundred pounds of morels a day, at an average of $3 to $4 per pound. Not bad for spending all day hiking in the woods, or a week in the wilderness. In the West, morels of different kinds like different types of soil, and they often flourish in an area the year after a wildfire. In those vast ranges, a morel hunter might encounter bear, moose, or snake. Once, my friend had a huge black bear run away from him, instead of toward him and his pack full of fresh mushrooms.

Back east in the safer Appalachians, my newly wed wife and I lived in a garage apartment at the end of a long, rocky driveway. Early one Saturday morning, three cars full of people pulled up, families of three or four generations. They exited their cars and spread through the grove of poplars behind our apartment, occasionally looking our way. Because we were the first people to inhabit this apartment, these "strangers" were as surprised to see us as we were to see them. It turned out that we were the interposers and that our visitors knew the landscape intimately, the kids heading out on their own, adults giving them quiet directions and then making sure the grandparents made it up the bank into the forest safely. I went out to see what they were doing and soon saw their full bags of morels, and knew: we found ourselves at the base of a huge morel patch that the local community had harvested for over a century. I picked a few mushrooms with them that day, watching, learning, and sharing my own stories about childhood morel hunts. Many of the pickers used canes, poking and turning over the leaves, always looking for the different texture, the four-inch mushrooms. As they left, I shook their hands and held on tight to the wrinkled hand of an eighty-nine-year-old woman born the same year as my deceased grandmother.

As a child, I rode in the backseat of my grandparents' big, blue Buick; we were headed to the mountain to hunt morels, a first for me. As soon as they stepped out of the car, both Grandpa and Grandma began filling their bread bags with the mushrooms. Grandpa gave me one so I knew what to look for, but still, the more I looked, the more I only saw last year's leaves. We spent billions of hours, it seemed, walking in circles around tulip poplar trees on Blue Mountain. After they each had filled their first bags and were working on their second, Grandma called me to her, saying, "I just saw one here, but lost it.

See if you can find it." I scanned and searched the tan ground, and finally, near her walking stick, I found my first morel.

That evening, after soaking them in saltwater to flush any tiny bugs, Grandma sautéed them in butter and then served us all a steaming plate full. I loved the earthy, salty, buttery taste, and my grandparents didn't seem to mind that I ate more than I found. I've been picking and eating ever since.

Have Fungi, But Be Careful

I always knew Smokey Bear had a sense of humor, despite his grim warnings about forest fires. On one of my favorite posters, he even smiles while wild, edible mushrooms grow from the brim of his hat. At the bottom, the benevolent old bear wisely advises, "Have fungi, but be careful."

One way to have fungi safely is to grow your own. While I enjoy harvesting wild morels and oyster mushrooms, I also enjoy growing and eating shiitakes. These mushrooms have been cultivated in China and Japan for over two thousand years, yet only recently have people in the West begun to enjoy these healthful—but not cheap—mushrooms. The going rate for fresh shiitake is around $3 per quarter pound, or $12 per pound. At your local farmers' market you can probably find them for around $8 per pound. But if you have some time and energy, and plain curiosity, consider growing your own. It's not too difficult, and with a little investment, you can reap a harvest for the next two to five years.

Making It Happen

To grow these delicacies, you first need some logs, prefer-ably oak, but other hardwoods will work. You'll need to move these logs periodically, so they can't be too heavy or big. The ideal width is four to six inches with a length of two to four feet, though I usually keep mine around three feet. Select fairly young, healthy trees that are alive and, if possible, in stands that need thinning. Winter is the ideal time to cut the logs because the heartwood is dense with sap, which makes for the best mushroom growing.

Inoculation is the process of getting the fungus spore into the log. Many methods for doing this exist, but the easiest is to drill holes and tap in wooden plugs with the spore already growing on them. I set the logs on saw-horses, use a 5/16-inch drill bit, and drill to a depth of about one and a quarter inches. Starting two to three inches from one end, I drill a ring of holes two to four inches apart around the log, and then move six to eight inches down the log to drill the next ring of holes. The last ring is two to three inches from the other end.

Next I gently hammer the plugs into these holes and then cover each with melted wax to seal in moisture and protect the spawn. A blow torch works well to heat a bar of wax which then drips into each plug. It's important to avoid contaminating logs with other fungi, so if possible, avoid dragging, and wash your hands frequently when handling the spawn.

After this hard part of inoculation is finished, move the logs to an outdoor shaded spot (60 percent or better, but not completely dark), with good ventilation and a source of water close by. Some people stack them in ricks, log-cabin style, but I lean them against a tree trunk or stack of lumber, with air space around each log.

The spawn will fully colonize a log within four to twelve months after inoculation. It won't die in cold weather, but when the temperature dips below forty-three degrees, it won't grow either. Spawn can die if the temperature exceeds one hundred degrees, so again, make sure the logs have plenty of shade and moisture.

You don't have to do much except check your logs every once in a while to see if they're fruiting. After wet weather, especially in the fall and spring, check them daily. Harvest the mushrooms when the edges are still curled under, usually when they are less than four inches in diameter. Harvest daily when they are fruiting.

This lazy method works, but not as well as if you control and force the fruiting more regularly. To do this, soak the logs for six to thirty-six hours in a bucket or tub, or even a stream or pond. When no bubbles appear on the surface, the log is fully saturated. Next "thump" the log by banging the end on the ground. No one knows for sure why this works, but it seems to increase the fruiting of each log. Some Asian growers even use mechanical vibrators.

Another factor in getting a log to fruit is temperature; forty to ninety degrees works best. Occasionally, I'll bring a log inside during the winter, soak it, keep it inside, and then have mushrooms to eat in a week or so. After this, a log that has just fruited must have at least two months to "rest" before you can force it to fruit again. An average log will bear approximately one pound per year for roughly four or five years (one year for every inch in diameter). These are only rules of thumb, though.

Fresh-picked mushrooms will keep one to two weeks in the fridge if kept in perforated plastic or waxed bags. They're best, though, within the first five days off the log. If you have an abundance all at once, shiitake are easy to dry and reconstitute for soups and casseroles.

In addition to tasting great, these mushrooms are extremely healthful, with many medical benefits. In *The Shiitake Way*, Dr. Andrew Weil recounts several medical studies that show how shiitake boost immunity, fight viruses, prevent heart disease, counteract fatigue and inflammation, and reduce serum cholesterol. Quite an impressive list for a fungus! This proves you can have fungi, be safe, and even be healthy, at the same time. For more information, including a recipe and a list of spawn suppliers, see the Appendix beginning on page 267.

The Bridge of Antlers

A few springs ago, while I trained my eyes on the treetops in search of migrating birds, our dogs focused on the ground, sniffing and circling an object buried in the leaf litter. They finally got my attention, and I went to take a look.

A deer antler lay buried in the grass, still full of enough curious smells to raise Becca's fur, our newly rescued pup not sure how close she could venture. I picked it up, felt the heft and miracle of this bone, and admired its beauty. It had four prongs, so it fell from a good-sized buck that probably knocked it off on a nearby sapling. I imagined him raising his back hoof to the top of his head, scratching the sore, and maybe even sighing in relief at shedding the extra weight.

Antlers truly are miracles. If you've found a dropped antler, you're lucky—it's a rare occurrence. And if you've ever held one, you know the weight. They are solid bone, substantial enough to knock another buck to the ground in a fight. A friend has a set of ten-point elk antlers someone shipped to him from Colorado. They weigh at least fifteen pounds and have a thirty-inch span and forty-inch height. I have trouble balancing them in my hands; I certainly can't imagine carrying them around on top of my head every year.

Antlers grow to these great sizes in four to five months, moose producing the biggest at sixty pounds. When a buck's new antlers are just coming in, they're covered with a velvety protective skin full of nutrients and blood vessels. In August, with the approach of mating season, the buck experiences a surge of testosterone, causing his antlers to harden as the blood stops flowing to them. When this happens, the velvet starts to peel, and the buck scratches his antlers on saplings to rub it off completely, creating the "buck rubs" so often visible in the woods. By February, the old antlers fall off, and the cycle starts again.

That antlers are the fastest-growing tissue known in the world may help to explain the possible medicinal properties of antler velvet. The Chinese have used it for over two thousand years, revering it almost as much as they do ginseng. Recent research, mainly in Russia and New Zealand, has found that the velvet improves the immune system, reduces the effects of stress, fights cancer, increases the production and circulation of blood, and—yes—enhances sexual energy. The Western scientific world still remains skeptical, but in reality, most of our current medicines come from nature (penicillin was discovered in bread mold, after all), so who knows the full medical value of antler velvet?

Humans have valued antlers in other ways as well for thousands of years. Donna and Cliff Boyd, anthropologists at Radford University, explain that "Native Americans used deer antler tines [as] pressure flakers for sharpening [stone] tool edges. The tines were also sometimes used as projectile points to tip spears or arrows." The Boyds have seen antlers "used as a handle for a stone knife," parts of a ceremonial mask, and most fascinating, as sewing needles. "Prehistoric peoples . . . would soak antler to soften it and split it with stone implements to get antler slivers for making needles and awls for sewing."

Though we don't sew with antler slivers today, human hands still transform these curved and tined bones into all sorts of furniture, decoration, and jewelry. A friend even saw a toothbrush made with an antler. My brother-in-law, like our prehistoric ancestors, made a knife handle out of one he found. And from the antler that the dogs sniffed out on our farm, Sarah later made a basket handle.

In the woods that day the dogs sniffed this mystery, I held the antler a long time, turned it over, and felt its smooth grace. I rubbed my thumb along the nibbled etchings where mice had gnawed, scratching the smooth white for nutrients. That antler arched like a bridge between my hands, a connection between our human history and this magnificent animal.

Growing Ginseng

Woodland herbs have been harvested from the wild for centuries, ginseng especially. In the late 1700s when ginseng covered the forest floor, Daniel Boone dug and bought several tons of roots—all of which he lost when his boat grounded in the Ohio River. Undaunted, and knowing that ginseng grew thick in the shady mountains, Boone traveled back upriver the next year and refilled his boat with another harvest. Today, because ginseng is near extinction in the wild, that boatload would be worth millions of dollars.

Overharvesting has all but destroyed wild patches of ginseng. The same has happened in the past decade with goldenseal, another powerful medicinal herb of the forest, and recently, the same is beginning to happen with black cohosh. All three once flourished in our Appalachian mountains, and with some work and luck, all three can be grown in any shady, moist woods. But I want to focus on the most sought-after, and hence, most expensive: ginseng.

The Chinese have taken ginseng medicinally for five thousand years, and modern research is finally confirming its value. Called an adaptogen, ginseng helps the body regulate its metabolism, adapt to stress, and find a healthy equilibrium.

The most prized ginseng roots are those grown in the wild. As one grower put it, "They should grow to look like they've been in pain." The gnarly, dark tan, and often forked roots sold for $350-450 per dried pound in 2000. That price continues to steadily increase because the demand is so strong for wild ginseng, especially plants grown "virtually wild" in woodlands.

Making It Happen

If you're interested in starting your own ginseng patch, a moist, well-drained hillside that faces north or east is the best location for planting. Seek dense shade of at least 75 percent from a canopy of hardwoods, like tulip poplar, sugar maple, and basswood. Ginseng has been grown on south-facing hillsides under pine, but that is usually too hot, dry, and densely shaded. Other plants that often thrive near ginseng—indicating a good spot to grow your own—include maidenhair fern, bloodroot, black cohosh, blue cohosh, Dutchman's pipe, and rattlesnake fern.

In midsummer, prepare to plant your ginseng by doing a soil test and ordering stratified seed from a reputable grower. Stay away from cheap seed and seed grown in Wisconsin which has a long history of disease problems. A pound of seed contains six to seven thousand seeds and costs anywhere from $50-100.

Plant in fall, and don't till. Instead, rake back the leaves in five-foot-wide beds that go down the hillside. You should try to simulate how ginseng grows in the wild, so don't "clean" these beds of trees or other plants. The less you disturb the soil, the better. Likewise, having a diversity of other plants close by decreases disease pressure.

Scratch three shallow trenches one inch deep down the length of each bed (eighteen inches apart) and then plant the ginseng seeds by hand so they are three inches apart in the furrow. Cover with three-quarters of an inch of soil, apply gypsum or rock phosphate as needed (depending on your soil test results), then rake one inch of leaves back over the bed. About one ounce of seed will plant a five-by-fifty-foot bed; one pound will plant roughly a tenth of an acre.

Two other planting methods are worth mentioning. Syl Yunker, a grower in Kentucky, has developed a planting stick which looks like a walking stick with a small-diameter pipe taped down the side and an old hunting knife taped to the bottom end. He uses the knife to poke a hole, drops a seed or two down the pipe, and then stamps it shut with his foot.

Still another method seems to be the fastest and easiest. A grower in North Carolina told me how he simply scatters the seed on the surface of the woods; then, with a garden rake, gently scratches the leaf litter back and forth, working the seed down under this mulch. Once the seeds have disappeared, he moves to the next spot. This sounds incredibly easy, and I hope to give it a try soon.

Once in the ground, ginseng takes anywhere from six to ten years to reach maturity, so once you've planted your patch, you can watch your calluses disappear for seven or so years. But it is definitely worth your time to make regular visits to each patch. According to Andy Hankins, the Virginia Extension specialist for alternative agriculture, "The greatest threat to a crop of wild-simulated ginseng is human theft." Our southern Appalachian culture still believes that "digging sang" is everyone's right, no matter who owns the land. Though I admire the art of "wildcrafting," I don't respect trespassing and stealing. The best defenses for your patch include secrecy, loud dogs, bulls (if your patch is surrounded by pasture), and mowing down the plant tops before they turn yellow in late summer.

When the patch is ready to harvest, dig up the roots in early fall. Hankins points out that "it takes nearly three hours to dig up three pounds of fresh roots that shrink to one pound of dried ginseng." That amount of time alone will slow any thieves from decimating a planting. Dry your roots, and then call any of the buyers in your region. Shop for the best price, and go cash in on this green gold.

For more information on ginseng, see the Appendix beginning on page 267.

A "Woods Garden"
Full of Cohosh

We hike up a huge mountain on a friend's property, following an old wagon road. After a mile of hiking straight up, we reach the top and soon find ourselves in what she calls her "woods garden." There, a thousand feet above her house, in a glade of century-old poplar and oak, we stand in a half acre thick with black cohosh. For several years, she has cultivated this woodland medicinal herb, spreading seed and breaking apart roots to replant. The five-foot-tall stems fill the understory, their seedpods rattling where once the white plumes flowered. The feathery leaves mix with maidenhair fern and spicebush.

My friend wants to thin one patch, so we dig into the black soil. I've never done this, so I scratch the earth tentatively with my fingers, to avoid injuring the roots. My friend instructs me to follow the dying stem two inches down, where I uncover a knot half the size of my fist, a black tuber full of root hairs. Carefully I dig around it and then, with a shovel, pry loose the root ball. When the earth releases, I'm holding a spider-shaped handful of powerful medicine.

We divide some of the roots into five or six rootlets and replant them in another section of woods. Some we harvest, for her to use and to sell. For every root we take, we break off the best bud and replant, our way of saying grace and harvesting sustainably. As a thank–you for helping, she gives me twelve roots of this beautiful herb to take home.

Woodland herbs have been harvested from the wild for centuries, and today, wild patches of ginseng and goldenseal have all but been destroyed by overharvesting. Now, the same is happening with black cohosh. In 1998, one broker of medicinal herbs bought an average of 140,000 plants per week. As benign as the term sounds, "wildcrafting" at this rate will soon destroy the cohosh population.

Why is black cohosh becoming overharvested? According to Richo Cech, an herb farmer and board member of United Plant Savers, "Black cohosh root is experiencing a current resurgence of popularity due to its application in treating pre-menstrual syndrome, menopause, estrogen deficiency, . . . and some kinds of depression." Steven Foster and James Duke, authors of *The Peterson Field Guide to Medicinal Plants*, agree. "Research has confirmed estrogenic, hypoglycemic, sedative, and anti-inflammatory activity. Root extract strengthens female reproductive organs in rats."

Back home with my gift of cohosh roots, I cut the fibrous masses into pieces, each with a bud ready to sprout in the spring. Since no black cohosh grows in our woodland, I plot out six different areas over the whole farm. Each plot is in a hardwood stand, but each differs in terms of shade, soil, and tree species. I want to see where this herb grows best. In the future, I'll propagate these plants to expand our "woods garden," and like the bumblebees, I'll enjoy the white plumes of flowers glowing in the deep summer shade.

For more information on cohosh and other medicinal herbs, see the Appendix beginning on page 267.

Wineberries—Wild, Red Jewels

On a hike up Rockcastle Gorge several years ago, Sarah and I filled our bellies with as many wineberries as we could pick. By dumb luck, we'd found the largest patch I'd ever seen, over an acre in the height of its July ripeness. With the music of the Carolina wren and the tumbling waters around us, we ate these jewels until we could hold no more, coming home with lips stained wineberry red.

The wineberry looks much like the red raspberry, each bramble made up of several individual bubbles of fruit. But the resemblances end there. The wineberry's red canes have thorns much less likely to snag you in the drawers. The thorns actually look like fine hair. The berries themselves ripen to a bright red, unlike the red raspberry's purplish color. Wineberries also have a firmer texture and freeze much better than their more delicate cousins. Most importantly, the taste of wineberries makes my mouth water just writing this. To me, red raspberries are almost too sweet. I enjoy eating them, but not in great handfuls like I consume wineberries and blueberries. I prefer a little more acid to cut the sweetness, a balance of flavors to relish.

This bramble originated in China or Japan and has spread throughout North America. But only after loving it for a few years did I fully learn of its invasive habits. I had watched it slowly spread down a hollow with each flood, but I hadn't realized that it was like coltsfoot, tree of heaven, and other exotic plants, crowding out the native spicebush and bluebells.

So how do you resolve this moral dilemma? How do you have your wineberry and eat it too? With a shovel, of course. I dug up three of the massive root balls closest to some Virginia bluebells; I wanted to save both berry and flower. These roots found a new home in our yard where I plan to control their spread while also harvesting their fruit; a foolish compromise, maybe, but a working one for now. The bluebells seem to appreciate the new space, and I will enjoy a ready supply of sweet, red jewels.

Until these transplants bear, I regularly suit up in long pants and rubber boots, put on chaps in case of copperheads, and head out for our secret patch. The dogs know the way, snarfing out the rabbit trails under all the brambles. But Little B, our shepherd/husky mix, hangs close by. She too likes these berries, sometimes pulling ripe and unripe berries off the vine. But usually she sits nearby and waits for me to feed her. Her tongue, like my own, carries the sweet stain of red as we hike back home.

In Praise of Pawpaws

During the fall of every year, Sarah and I make a pilgrimage to the pawpaw patch. We journey down the mountain to our friends' farm in Shawsville where the wild pawpaws flank the Roanoke River in abundance. With buckets, we cross the low-water bridge and enter the grove, picking as we please, and always filling our stomachs with this incredibly sweet fruit, the largest edible fruit native to the United States.

The taste of a pawpaw is often compared to that of its tropical cousins, the banana and mango, with a hint of strawberry. I just like the mushy sweetness and custard-like texture that squeezes out of the skin. And the best way to eat them is fresh off the tree. That's one reason you won't find any in the grocery produce section. The pawpaw has little, if any, "shelf life," and only in recent years have researchers begun to develop it as a commercial crop. So, if you want to eat this "poor man's banana," you need to find a patch, or plant a few trees of your own.

Making It Happen

In the wild, these low-growing understory trees usually congregate near water, so begin your search there. Look for ten- to twenty-foot trees with huge, oblong leaves that often hide the fruit. The fruit itself hugs the branches in clusters and looks like giant, green kidney beans, the largest about four inches long and weighing one pound. A shake of the skinny trunk brings down the clusters, and if the skin has turned brown, the pawpaw is ripe and ready to eat. Just rip it in half, squeeze out a bite, slurp it up, and spit out the seeds.

Or, hold onto the seeds—large, brown, bean-like nuggets—and propagate your own pawpaw patch. We saved over one hundred from last year, keeping them in the fridge for about three months to stratify them. Then over Christmas break, I planted the seeds in pots, hoping for success. I didn't weed or water them, as I should have through the dry summer, but a few still emerged. Slow to germinate, they only began to break into the light in July or August. So far, I have about fifteen seedlings, and I probably won't see any fruit from these for another six to eight years.

A more predictable way to ensure your own harvest is to plant a grove of mail-order seedlings. Many nurseries now offer them at roughly $15-20 each. Make sure they come with a guarantee, and consider buying potted seedlings since pawpaws are notoriously difficult to pro-pogate. Once mature, these pyramid-shaped trees will bear beautiful, maroon-colored blooms in the spring, and with ample pollination, plenty of fruit in the fall.

Three tips to make sure you get fruit: shade the seedlings their first year or two; plant at least two for cross-pollination; and when the trees are ready to bear, hang "road-kill" in their branches. Seriously! Pawpaw blooms smell like carrion, and by stringing a dead possum to a limb, you attract the right type of carrion flies, which do the pollination work for you. Just don't let the neighbors see, or smell, what you're up to.

I've searched most of my home county of Floyd for native stands, without any luck. I'm guessing the late frosts have hindered them from spreading into our area. But other enthusiasts across the country are finding more and more native stands, and scientists have planted several research groves, especially in Kentucky. And of course, I encourage you to join the Pawpaw Foundation. One of their recent newsletters included a member list, an update on plantings in eleven states, and a story about an Ohio business that sells frozen pawpaw pulp to restaurants across the country. Last year this company processed over 2,500 pounds of pawpaws—not too shabby for the "poor man's banana"!

To find out how to contact the Pawpaw Foundation, visit the Appendix beginning on page 267.

Growing

Food Security, or Do You Know Where That Egg Came From?

Imagine your most recent meal sitting on a table before you. Let's say it's breakfast. Now pick one of the ingredients, maybe an egg, and trace its journey back to the chicken. How far did you get?

I've done this exercise often with Radford University classes, and the trail of the egg almost always grows cold in the nearest grocery store's dairy section. Like most of us, these students don't know how far that egg traveled, where the chicken lived, or how the chicken was treated. Like most of us, my students don't know the source of their food, and often, they don't care.

But care we all should with the growing concerns about food security, health, and the environment. A 1983 study found that the average food item in the United States travels 1,300 miles before it reaches the dinner table. Given NAFTA and the globalization of our economy, that number surely has increased. How often have you brought a bag of Chilean grapes home from the grocery store in the dead of winter? More importantly, how much ecological damage occurred with the mere shipment of that produce? And what are the human costs of this vast food distribution system? We would be horrified if someone sabotaged a shipment of beef, tainted it with *e coli*, and caused thousands of people to get sick and die. A scary proposition, but it regularly happens by accident because our food system is so gigantic and geared toward efficiency, speed, and money.

Take that breakfast egg, for example. As a teenager, I worked at my best friend's farm. His dad operated a layer house, a windowless factory longer than a football field that held over sixty thousand birds. Each white chicken lived in a three-foot-square cage with eight other noisy birds, sandwiched between other cages beside, above, and below. The eggs rolled out on a conveyer belt, the food rolled in on a different belt, and the droppings fell into a ten-foot pit.

At the time, I thought little of the birds' plight. I was more fascinated with the German-speaking Amish girls who worked beside me. Later, though, I began to realize all of the problems with such a large-scale industry. These clucking creatures never saw the sun, never scratched the earth, never even enjoyed a dirt bath. They were pumped with antibiotics to prevent diseases. And instead of spreading their own feces over a pasture, they simply had to let it drop below them. Imagine sleeping, eating, breathing, just plain living with 59,999 other creatures above a year's worth of your own shit.

It doesn't have to be like this. Our eggs can come from local farmers, our lettuce from a nearby market gardener instead of a California mega-farm. Our region still has an agricultural tradition, and our population centers are still small enough that local farms could supply many of our needs. Imported oranges and avocados would become true luxuries instead of the everyday miracles we take for granted. If we valued health and security more than wealth, we could begin this process of becoming more self-sufficient, and in turn, create healthier local economies.

One of the first steps would be ascertaining what assets we already have. In Watauga County, North Carolina, a class taught at Appalachian State University spent a semester creating an "Asset-Based Map" of the county. They interviewed local farmers, suppliers, and marketers, and then listed them in an index to show the many food assets that already existed. The class also examined the agricultural education and cultural assets, diagramming the connections and resources available, as well as the barriers. They found the main barriers to be poorly planned land development, the dying out of the farmer, and industrialization—the same issues faced across our country.

Other schools have taken the process of local food security a step further. At the University of Northern

Iowa, thanks to a grant, students have become interns at area institutions like hospitals and nursing homes. The intern's job is to find local food for each institution, making connections between farmer and chef. In California, also through grants, many of the public schools now produce a portion of their own food in school gardens. Local farmers, who often visit the classes, produce much of the rest of each school's food.

We can do this, but not with ease. The existing system already gears itself against buying locally. Our state universities, for example, are governed by laws which require volumes of paperwork and capital, usually eliminating the local farmer. But laws can change, and so can people.

Though less than 2 percent of our population farms, we all eat. We affect the earth the most, not by what we drive or wear, but by what we eat, by how and where that food is grown. We make choices every time we take a bite, and often we are ignorant of each mouthful's effects on the earth and ourselves. If we eat from the sustainable table, we buy local produce of higher quality, we pollute much less, and we protect the soil, water, and air, as well as our farming neighbors and our own food security. Consider this at your next meal.

Grow a Patch of Your Own

I wanted to put in a small patch of strawberries, and I figured my best source of information was my next-door neighbor, John Sutherland. John has grown strawberries for pick-your-own customers for over forty-five years. We both live "back in" the remote Alum Ridge section of Floyd County, but every June, the traffic on our dirt road increases from five cars a day to a hundred and five. The customers stream in from all over southwest Virginia, and even North Carolina and West Virginia. They come for John's incomparably sweet, fresh berries, and to visit a little, and if they're lucky, to hear John sing and play the piano.

When I began to visit John, he first made sure I wasn't going to compete in the business. I assured him that mine was only a patch for my family and that we wanted to try growing berries organically. He rolled his eyes at the organic part (we have an ongoing debate over this), but John graciously started to share his wisdom, compiling his years of experience into two short hours.

Making It Happen

I learned from John that the best ground is in full sun, high in organic matter and newly cleared. Sod land will have a lot of white grubs, so treat it with chemicals. A county extension agent can offer advice for selecting the best chemical treatment; milky spore disease, an organic bacteria that kills grubs, can also be used. Avoid frost pockets or ground that has recently grown tomatoes or potatoes, because these plants harbor verticillium wilt, which is deadly to strawberries. John also said to "avoid land infested with deer"; they continue to be a major problem for him, eating his plants through the long winter.

If possible, plow your plot to a depth of six to eight inches in the fall or early in the spring, but avoid working with too-wet soil. Be sure to have a soil test to see what nutrients you need to add, and again, consult the extension agent for advice. John recommends fertilizing with 10-10-10 at five hundred pounds per acre, but I plan to use the equivalent amounts of organic fertilizer, like bloodmeal and rock phosphate. Broadcast your fertilizer in the spring and work it in with a rake or spring-tooth harrow.

Next choose your plants. John stressed the importance of the origin of your plants. The best are certified virus-free and are as free of other diseases and insects as possible. John's had good success with plants from nurseries in Maryland.

One of his favorite varieties is Red Chief because of its resistance to leaf and soil diseases. He also has had success with Earliglow, Lateglow, Sparkle, Allstar, Surecrop, and Guardian. Each of these varieties will produce good-tasting berries, but each also has its individual problems, like susceptibility to diseases, intolerance of drought, or a decrease in productivity after the first season. Many successful growers plant small plots to see which varieties yield the best berries in their location, and you'd be wise to follow their lead.

Once you receive your plants, get them in the ground as soon as possible. If the soil is too wet or frozen, hold them over in your refrigerator until conditions improve. Plant each to the right depth. John emphasized this repeatedly. "The crown (the base of the plant) must be flush with the soil level," he said, "not too shallow or too deep." This ensures that the runners will extend outward, and the plant will propagate and thrive. Once the plant is in the soil, tamp the dirt with your feet turned inward, toward the plant, to make all of the air pockets disappear.

Space plants two to three feet apart in rows four feet apart. If you plan to irrigate, increase this spacing because strawberries can really spread with adequate moisture. If you plan to depend on rainfall for moisture, as John had for forty years, "consult your local minister," to use his phrase. The plants just don't like dry conditions.

About six weeks after you set out the new plants, start picking off all the blooms. This sends the energy into the root system and creates a vigorous heavy-bearer. Pinch the blooms or snip them off with scissors, as pulling them off will hurt the mother plant.

The other big job the first year is controlling the weeds by cultivating around the plants. But be careful not to cut into the berry's root system.

Strawberries are afflicted with several devastating leaf diseases, including leaf spot, leaf scorch, and powdery mildew. They're also susceptible to soil diseases like verticillium wilt and red stele. Choose varieties resistant to these diseases, like the ones mentioned above, and also be ready, if you're not committed to growing organically, to spray regularly. Again, consult your county agent for recommended sprays. Use straw mulch, if possible, to cover the plants during the winter. This can then be pulled back in the spring, and the straw will help prevent the spread of diseases which splash up from the ground.

After all of this hard work and a year of waiting, you'll see a patch of "white blooms like snow"—as John described them—in mid-May. Soon after this, you'll have ripe, red berries to pick and eat, and if any remain, freeze. To get the best flavor, pick only those which are fully red and ripe—and pick daily.

Once they stop bearing, mow the strawberry plants. This rejuvenates the patch and causes the plants to grow vigorously and bear well the next season. In fact, John noted, "Each week after July 4 that you don't mow, you lessen the next year's crop by one-fourth." So, mow *before* July 4. Set the mower at one inch above the ground, making sure not to mow the crown—just the leaves. Fertilize with a source of nitrogen to give these plants a needed boost.

Even if you harvest a bumper crop of these red jewels, you can still learn a lot about techniques and varieties by visiting your local pick-your-own farm this June. Sad to say, though, you won't be able to pick at John's; because of the deer and his health, John Sutherland has decided not to grow any more strawberries. He and I are both going to miss the happy hands of visitors picking his fields clean.

To learn more about growing your own fresh strawberries, see the Appendix beginning on page 267.

Some Kind of Habit

I started as a teen, and I still can't break this habit. The painful inhaling that brings tears, the relief that comes after the initial sting—all this I can't give up. My grandparents, of all people, got me addicted to this white root that grinds to a powder, this habit of loving horseradish.

One winter evening, my grandmother told me to get the shovel out of the milkhouse. From there, we walked to the side of the yard and a bare patch of earth. "Dig right there," she pointed with her cane, her arthritic knees stiffened to straightness. I dug around in the dirt, found the yellowish-white root, and pulled it out. "That's what we want," said Grandma.

In the kitchen, Grandpa waited at the sink where he scrubbed and peeled the root. I watched as first Grandma, then Grandpa, turned the crank of the old meat grinder, pushing the root in the top chute, watching the pulp trickle out the bottom, holding their breath for twenty turns, then scurrying to the door for fresh air. After his third trip to the door, tears welling in his eyes, Grandpa nodded his head toward the grinder and told me to try. The fumes had filled the kitchen, but I wasn't crying as they were, yet. I turned the wooden knob three times and then looked down into the top to see how much of the root had disappeared. I also inhaled. Tears blurred the room, and I stumbled to the door while my grandparents' chuckles filled my ears. They finished the grinding, and even on that cold winter evening, we kept the door open.

These days I use a blender to grind my roots, but still, I cry every time. Horseradish's volatile oil kicks ten times harder than any onion and is a great sinus clearer if you have a cold, or even if you don't. But this pungent perennial herb, once ground, has a short shelf life, so add a little vinegar, keep it sealed in the refrigerator, and eat it within two to three weeks. Even at three weeks old, though, it has more flavor and kick than store-bought, and it still adds punch to toasted cheese sandwiches, roast beef, or my grandparents' favorite, shrimp cocktail sauce.

Making It Happen

Horseradish easily propagates from root cuttings. In fact, for some gardeners, it becomes a weed, so pay attention to where you start your patch, preferably in a garden corner, or some place it can spread without becoming a pest. You can purchase pencil-sized starter rootlets from any of several seed companies, or maybe you can help thin a friend's patch. Extension Agent Andy Hankins recommends spacing these cuttings every twenty-four inches in rows thirty inches apart. Plant in April and May, and fertilize lightly with compost or aged manure. Since the root can grow up to a foot or more in length, plant it in deep, moist, but well-drained soil with a relatively neutral pH. It can tolerate some shade, and from my experience, it is pest-free. The rabbits slide under our garden fence, hop through the horseradish, and never bother it, preferring instead our beans a hundred feet away.

For large, straight roots that make for easier processing, Hankins explained that some growers trim the side shoots twice during the growing season. When the largest leaves reach eight inches, they pull the soil away from the top of the main root and strip the smaller rootlets off. They replace the soil and then do it again a month later. The result is a smooth root with few, if any, side shoots. I've never done this, but I'm curious if the extra work is worth the effort.

Grandma always told me you can harvest horseradish in any month that has an *r* in it, especially after a frost or two, and all the written sources agree with her. This makes storage easy. As Hankins asserts, "The best place to store horseradish roots through the winter is right out in the field where they have grown." If this isn't possible, the roots keep fairly well in sand in a root cellar, or in a bag in the crisper drawer in your refrigerator.

For the truly addicted, the crisper drawer is also a great storage place if you want to have a fresh supply through summer. Dig the roots before May, and then through the heat of summer, grind as needed to sustain your habit.

How to Get the Good Bugs In

"If you grow it, they will come." So says Richard McDonald, an entomologist who has studied bugs all of his life. His take on the famous line from *Field of Dreams* implies that if farmers and gardeners plant the right plants, the beneficial insects will come. I'm beginning to believe he might be right.

McDonald recently told me of a grower for Highland Lake Inn in Flat Rock, North Carolina, who had eliminated almost all pesticide use, organic and synthetic. The farmer, Patryk Battle, occasionally used soap spray in his greenhouse, but otherwise he applied no other controls, including the introduction of mail-order beneficials. How did Battle grow beautiful vegetables on over one and a half acres? How did he deal with the potato and bean beetles along with the squash vine borer, stink bugs, and other "pests"? If McDonald's right, Battle did it all with beneficial plants that attract, feed, and shelter the beneficial insects already present. Battle studied the needs of these great bugs and continually provided for them. I haven't seen Battle's garden, but I believe in the principle because I've seen successes like this on a smaller scale with our own plants.

In our blueberry field, for example, I've begun to change my attitude about one of our most persistent weeds. Red sorrel, a low-growing, tough-rooted creeper, has steadily covered several of our beds. Annoyed by it last year, I spent days weed-eating it into the ground, trying to chew up its very roots with the nylon string of the trimmer. I set it back a year, maybe, but I also chewed up our mulch, which decomposed in a season instead of the two years we expected.

But two ironies about this sorrel have changed my mind. The beds with the worst sorrel also bore the most berries. The sorrel, it seems, bothers us more than the bushes. The other irony I missed is that the sorrel crawls with lady beetles. This spring we counted twenty-five lady beetle larvae and adults in one square foot, all feasting on aphids and keeping the population of soft-bodied pests on the bushes in check. The sorrel will now get chopped down just once before pickers come at the end of June.

I've begun to favor other "weeds" also, as I read more and more on what attracts beneficial insects. Both in the garden and the blueberry field, I've allowed yarrow and Queen Anne's lace to grow undisturbed. Both plants have flowers used by a wide range of "good bugs."

Who are these "good bugs"? I'm still learning, but those most welcome in our field include lady beetles, green lace wings (who have green bodies with delicate, well-named wings), syrphid flies (hover flies), and parasitic wasps (tiny and harmless). These all eat or parasitize a wide variety of insects, especially aphids, small caterpillars, and scale. We have many beneficials now, but I want to attract more to the garden and field, to build and sustain this natural population. The trick to encouraging the "good bugs" to stick around is to always have something in bloom, plants that offer nectar, pollen, shelter, and other bugs to eat. This means allowing for more diversity and less pesticide use, including organic pesticides. Rotenone, a powerful organic pesticide, will kill many beneficials, so if you want to attract them, try to avoid all pesticides as much as possible.

In addition to Queen Anne's lace and yarrow, other plants I want to welcome to both garden and berry patch include anything in the carrot family (again, Queen Anne's lace, but also tansy, dill), anything in the sunflower family (sunflowers, coreopsis, cosmos, goldenrod), the clover family, brassicas and mustard gone to flower (don't pull those old broccoli plants; let them bloom!), and buckwheat and corn. Having something in bloom at any time will take a few years to accomplish, but as these plants grow, hopefully the beneficial insects will come to feast, sleep, and multiply forever. The good bugs can't play baseball like Kevin Costner's crew, but still it's worth creating the ideal field for these powerful sluggers.

Summertime, Winter Work

Winter works us. Even in the green, humid exuberance of midsummer, winter is a demanding boss. She doesn't pay in presidential portraits, but she does reward, if we only give her our attention.

In the garden, I pick summer's fruit with sweat dripping from my nose, the heat making me run to the pond for a dunking. The kitchen fills with steam from processing tomatoes and peaches, beans and corn. Around the dehydrator, the heated air takes on the scent of the drying apples and blueberries. The root cellar and freezer fill with the colors of summer, the jars lining up in an alphabet that spells health, energy, love. This bounty of an overflowing larder stored for the long, dark six months is one of winter's pleasures.

Like the root cellar, my notebook also gets filled with the fruit of summer stored for winter use. I am too busy during the blueberry season to write at length, so I jot ideas for poems and stories in a journal. Winter gives time to develop the stories about picking berries in the rain, or learning from pickers how to say "blueberry" in French or Korean.

Tomorrow I'll cut firewood, the chain saw biting off chunks of hardness, the sawdust filling my boot. I'll carry each chunk arm-load by arm-load to the woodshed, where the stacked rounds will look back at me, blank-faced, the white of maple, the different reds of cherry, apple, and oak. All year as I pass by, I touch this insurance of heat.

That reality—the heft of wood, the book of memories, the colorful pantry, all of it neatly stacked energy banked for the negative-fourteen-degree nights—that reality is winter's work and one of winter's many gifts.

Gray Buffalo

Thick clouds roll in across the prairie of the sky, like a herd of gray buffalo, their hooves rumbling louder and louder. When the thunder is too close, we yell for the pickers to come out of the blueberry field. I don't want to practice my rusty CPR on a pail-toting, lightning-struck customer.

A week earlier, a huge storm hit our farm three times, killing or damaging trees. The first knocked the top out of a scarlet oak at the edge of the field. The second hit a white pine, traveled twenty feet underground, then four feet up the trunk of another pine. The third killed a huge white oak at the back of our farm. The bark flew over 150 feet from the tree, the white inner wood exposed for the first time, an instant death for the hundred-year-old oak.

A few years ago, thunder and lightning didn't bother me. When we planted the blueberries, we worked through several heavy storms. One, I know now, I should have avoided. So massive and so close, it forever changed Grace, our collie. Before, lightning didn't bother her, but from then on, she cowered when the buffalo-rumbling approached.

Since then, I too have grown more cautious, more respectful, especially when I learned that a single bolt of lightning is three to five times hotter than the sun and can travel twenty miles. I'm amazed that any struck trees, or jolted people, even survive, yet most do. About a hundred people a year are killed by lightning, and that's roughly only 20 percent of all who are struck. Males account for over 80 percent of the unlucky targets. Either men have more electrical magnetism or are just more prone to think, "It can't happen to me."

But it does strike women as well. One woman, Gretel Ehrlich, writes of her experience in a beautiful and startling book entitled *A Match to the Heart*. She chronicles her struggles, from walking her dogs across a Montana pasture where she was struck, to the many medical problems that she now must endure: the most troubling, her heart slowing for no reason. She had to leave Montana for a lower elevation to try to regain her health.

When the gray buffalo roll across our blueberry field, I seek shelter now, watching the herd pass, waiting for safer wind and quieter sky.

Beans, Bovines, and Beetles

We grew up teasing our friends as they trudged home to another dreaded meal of beans ("Beans, beans, beans, the more you eat . . . "). Yet now, both Sarah and I love beans, baked, stewed, refried, chili-ed, and on and on.

Instead of buying several pounds of dried beans a year, we decided to grow and dry all we needed. The experiment proved so successful, we're still eating the legumes we grew several years ago.

To start, we weeded through all the glamorous catalog descriptions to choose five types that we knew we liked or thought we might. These include kidney for chili; pinto for soup; garbanzo for salad and sandwich spreads; black turtle for main dishes; and Jacob's Cattle for soup, and because they had a beautiful white and maroon coat.

We planted one pound of seed of each variety (across about a hundred feet of land), mulched and weeded, and tried to keep the Mexican bean beetles at bay by hand-picking. We also used rotenone once on the beetles, a botanical pesticide that unfortunately wipes out beneficial bugs as well as bad.

The rotenone seemed to control the bean beetles, but not the tough Japanese ones. Nor did it deter the neigh-

bor's cattle who trampled in through a broken gate.
These toothy Angus seemed to prefer the pinto and garbanzos, for some odd reason.

Except for the garbanzo, all the beans flourished,
blooming prolifically despite the bugs. The garbanzos,
I'm guessing, prefer a longer, warmer season, and definitely fewer cattle.

Three to four months later, after battling bovines and
beetles, we watched the plants wither and dry, their life
used up and now stored in a seed we wanted to eat. And
eat we would. On average, each variety yielded more
than ten pounds, giving us forty pounds total—enough
for a very long time.

Getting those forty pounds, however, took some room
and effort. The plants must be harvested before the seeds
fall from the pods, but they also need as much drying
time as possible. A good rule for harvesting: pick when
there are one or two green pods for every ten dry ones.
We found that pulling the whole plant and then stacking
in a leak-proof shed for another few weeks worked well
to allow for more drying. Then, as we had time, we
threshed and winnowed, both dusty jobs requiring a dust
mask, but also easy and interesting tasks.

To thresh, I cleaned off any remaining dirt on the
roots, held each plant by the root end, and beat it against

the inside of a clean garbage can. The threshing usually popped the seeds from the pods, though a few pods weren't dry enough and had to be opened by hand. Another method I've read about requires putting the plants in feed sacks and getting the neighborhood children to jump on them. Either method should work well.

For winnowing, another activity kids would enjoy, I used two clean buckets and a large fan. On porch steps, I poured the beans from one bucket to the other in front of the running fan. The air blew away the chaff, separating out the edible beans. Depending on how cleanly we harvested the beans, I also needed to sort through them to discard pebbles and small clumps of dirt that passed through the winnowing process.

The beans required two more steps, both easy. First, I spread them out on a sheet or tray in a warm, dry room for a week or so until they had fully dried. Test for dryness with the shatter technique. Hammer a few beans. If they smoosh, they're not dry enough. If they shatter, they're ready for the next step.

Once the drying process was complete, we poured the beans into mason jars for storage and froze the many colored nuggets for four or five days to kill any lurking bean weevils (bean weevils can quickly destroy the whole crop). Once in storage, beans will keep their nutritional value for four years, maybe longer. So all the effort can pay off for quite some time.

One other note: a year or two after we grew these different varieties, liking them all, a friend introduced us to a different variety, the adzuki. It too makes a fine soup, chili, or main dish, with the added benefit of not being bothered as much by Mexican bean beetles. They don't seem to like its hairy stems. Because of this, the small, good-tasting adzuki has become our primary dried bean.

Groundhogs

I inherited my hate for groundhogs from Grandpa. He instilled in me, while I was still young, his utter disgust for those hairy varmints that live in holes. We both disliked the "hogs," as we called them, because they ate our alfalfa, or if they were daring, they'd sneak into our garden and feast on our beans or cantaloupes or tomatoes. They were tricky animals in collusion with the devil.

We hated them most, though, because of the placement of their holes. The "hogs" forever wanted to dig three or four in the middle of every one of our hayfields; they weren't comfortable living on the edges. Den-building in the center of the fields created havoc when we worked there—like the time I was fifteen and we were baling hay. Grandpa avoided the groundhog holes with the tractor and baler, but the wagon hit a hole, throwing Uncle Harry and me clear off. Grandpa just swore a long blue line at that groundhog, then spit his tobacco in the hole.

When I was twelve and an expert with my BB gun, Grandpa gave me permission to use his .22s. I set a target in the pasture, and he taught me how to load and shoot the .22 magnum that had a scope. I hit the bull's eye three out of five times, and Grandpa figured I could use the gun.

The next day, off I went to hunt groundhogs. I soon realized that there was more to hunting than shooting well. I learned the patience needed for sitting on a hill above a den and waiting an hour for the critters to emerge; or the stealth needed to slip through a cornfield and surprise the animals who sunned themselves in the open hayfield; or the anger of missing the same ground-hog three straight times, and the blood-tinged joy of finally finding my mark and dropping the dead wood-chuck back into his hole.

On a locust fence post next to the barn, Grandpa and I would keep tallies for each summer, scratching with our pocketknives who killed the most groundhogs. My record was eight and his, a dozen. But even killing twenty in one summer didn't slow their spread into our fields. One summer when he got fed up with our losing battle, Grandpa bought smoke bombs. For the next two days, we drove from infested field to infested field. I covered all the side holes with burlap sacks, and he lit the smoke bomb and threw it down the main entrance, which I then covered with another sack. The smoke burned my eyes and made us both cough, but we knew these were small sacrifices in our battle. A month later, after we hadn't seen any groundhogs, we declared our victory. The next summer, however, we saw fresh dirt around their holes and knew we'd never win.

Years later I have been relearning that I'll never "beat" groundhogs. For eight years, I didn't handle a gun. In that time, I went off to college, then worked in other places, and I found that guns and killing went against the grain of my stock. But this summer's garden changed that. We put in a large garden in the original homestead plot. When the beans started sprouting, we discovered groundhogs with voracious appetites living under the surrounding briers. They regularly snack on tomatoes and beans and, in one weekend, have eaten five heads of cabbage and eight heads of broccoli. Nothing is beyond their toothy touch: birdhouse gourds, watermelons, even prized cantaloupes. I had ten melons in various stages of growth, and a day later, before they were even ripe, I only had five.

To combat these varmints, I've tried just about every-thing. The only device that's worked is Mom's old panty-hose slipped over the melons; the groundhogs don't seem to like the taste of nylon. For the peas, beans, and toma-toes, I've put up chicken wire, which the critter crawls under. I regularly yell obscenities from the porch and piss around the garden border, to no avail.

Frustrated, I finally got my .22 from home, a Marlin open-sight that Grandpa bought just before he died. It's a good gun, but over the years, I've become a bad shot, especially when I don't have a scope to help. I've killed two groundhogs in the last three months and have missed more than I care to admit. The first one I killed was a youngster at point-blank range. He didn't know to run from me. The second was full-grown and fat from eating our beans. For two weeks, I shot at him and missed several times. Finally I set a target in the garden and practiced shooting. I figured out the sights and killed the groundhog the next day.

But still, two old warriors somehow always know when I'm not home, or when I am home and shooting, they know I'm a bad shot.

Next spring I plan to build a better fence and bury the bottom six inches. If Grandpa were still alive, he'd say I should forget the fence and just shoot the damn things.

And maybe he's right.

Health, Hunger, and Hunting

"The supermarket is an agent of our forgetfulness."
—Richard Nelson, *Heart and Blood*

Once I was a vegetarian. My poor mother had fits trying to fix tofu-broccoli bonanza for me and chicken for the rest of the family. We eyed each other's plates suspiciously because for the first time, food divided us instead of joined us. I just ate my silky tofu in moral solitude.

I didn't eat meat for many reasons, but mainly because of health—mine and the world's. I knew the dangers of too much meat, but I was more bothered by the worldwide unequal distribution of food. If we ate the grain, instead of the grain-fed animal, more people would have the possibility of more food, more water, and a healthier environment. The animals, too, would have a better life. The rest of my family, though, still ate their beef and chicken.

I used to join them, relishing the juicy steak or fried chicken leg. Eventually, I came to understand the ecological tragedy I participated in with each bite. I read about the cattle yards in the Midwest filled with thousands of bovines standing knee-deep in their own manure. In

North Carolina, the state with more pigs than people, I saw pig factories, their manure lagoons bursting, killing the rivers with their brown stench. I watched documentaries about the working conditions in slaughterhouses, heard the stories of women who processed ninety chickens an hour, often losing fingers, often losing jobs when their hands couldn't handle the cold water and repetition anymore. Though I loved meat, I couldn't support this type of food system. So I stopped eating flesh for ten years and learned to love tofu.

About the same time I became a vegetarian, I stopped hunting. It seemed the next logical step. I grew up hunting, even enjoyed target practice, but I always feared the power of a gun. Every fall, my dad, uncles, and I fanned across the farm, kicking up rabbits and shooting pheasants. I enjoyed the camaraderie, the walkabouts, the jokes and teasing, but never the weight of the limp bird, never the blood and naked body of a skinned rabbit.

In the cold of November, we hunted deer, and I never could stop shivering enough to shoot one. That and I'd fall asleep. Once a doe's swishing steps woke me after she ran within two feet of where I dozed. She stopped when she caught my scent, turned around to look, then flounced her tail and snorted away. I headed to the truck to warm my numb fingers.

I helped butcher several but never killed a deer, never had a good shot. That all changed recently, after not handling a rifle for twenty years.

Two years ago, deer grazed our garden greens and nibbled on our acre of blueberries, our cash crop, our income. The game warden walked our field and knew we had no other effective and cheap control for such a large area. He issued a special permit allowing us to kill ten out of season. He saw the deer's overpopulation and said to let him know if we needed another permit.

I was not ready to hunt yet, not confident in my marksmanship, or clear on my thinking about eating meat or killing, but I knew if I wanted to farm, I could not do nothing. I called Paul, my brother-in-law, and surprised him by asking him to hunt on our farm. He readily agreed and drove the three hours from Charlotte the next weekend.

Over the course of that winter, Paul killed two does and a yearling that still had its spots. Sarah and I sat in our house, waiting for the gun blasts, and still we jumped when they echoed through the hollow.

After the first shot, when his headlights signaled his success, I drove to the field to help him dress the doe. By headlight, we hoisted her from a tree and carefully cut open her beautiful, gray-brown fur. Mostly Paul cut, and I held the flashlight. The insides slowly piled on the ground, and then when all was loose, the stomach, lungs, and intestines spilled out. We cut and pulled the hide off, fisting it from the fat and muscle. Our hands grew slick with her fat and blood. Steam from her body mixed with our own breath.

The next summer, two people opened a new space in my mind for hunting, showed that doing one's own killing was the most ecologically responsible way to live. At a conference Gary Paul Nabhan explained his eating dilemma. He realized that not our paper usage, not even our cars, but our agriculture causes the most environmental damage. To change this on a personal level, he sought to eat 80 percent of his diet from within 250 miles of his home. Additionally, to preserve local diversity, he wanted 90 percent of this food to be native and local in origin. Nabhan's practice circumvents the massive marketing, packaging, refrigeration, transportation, and genetic engineering systems that bring us food.

I met Richard Nelson at the same conference and later read his book, *Heart and Blood: Living With Deer in North America*. An anthropologist who lived for several years with natives in Alaska, Nelson traced his own transformation in relation to hunting—from an urbanite anti-hunter, to a hunter who respects his prey, who "loves deer, not only as wild, beautiful creatures, but also as a source of [his] own existence; as animals who elevate [his] senses, enrich [his] spirit, and nourish [his] body." Nelson also showed that my vegetarian ways still involved killing deer. No matter how far I tried to distance myself from killing, the killing still took place, whether or not I partici-pated directly. According to Nelson, "Everyone in North America who lives on agricultural food belongs to an eco-logical network that necessarily involves deer-hunting." The deer population has exploded so much that in much of the United States today, "hunting is no less important to farmers than is the plow."

Both Nabhan and Nelson forced me to analyze my own "personal ecology." Would I do more damage to this earth by eating an organic carrot from California or a wild deer from my own backyard? The heart-shaped print in our garden showed me the answer.

At 5:30 a.m. on opening day, Paul and I head to oppo-site hills. I carry my dad's 30.06 rifle, one I sighted in a month ago, after target practicing with a .22. In the dark-ness of pre-dawn, I startle a creature that crashes away. I cut across the blueberry field to a spot in the spring hollow I picked out earlier. By a sassafras tree, I clear away leaves and try to check my views, both down the wooded slope toward our spring and behind to the top of the hill. Even though I can't see through the darkness, I know several deer paths cross nearby, so I wait.

A half hour later, the light just opening the woods, I hear a crashing of branches from uphill. I slowly turn, click off the safety, and remember to breathe. The footsteps stop, and there, between pines, a silhouette appears. In my scope I see the dainty legs, the head bending down trying to catch my scent, aware of danger. I pull the trigger and a flash fills the space between us. My ear rings, and I run to where her footsteps stop. Twenty feet from where the bullet pierced her heart, fifty feet from where I stood, I find the large doe dead under a pine. Kneeling beside her, I make sure she is dead and catch my breath. And then I pray, thankful for a safe hunt, for a clean shot, and most of all, for this body, this death that will give me life.

That deer filled our freezer, and, as I slowly gave up my vegetarian ways, each bite tied me more closely to this place we call home. Each meal forced me to remember the dashing brown bodies, white tails wagging through the woods whenever we startled each other, or the doe that entered our yard in the summer, a chestnut-colored beauty whose big eyes warily looked our way as we hid behind a curtain. She ate our grass, graced our afternoon, then flicked her tail and faded into the pines.

Each bite binds me to the heart-shaped hoofprints on the muddy bank of the pond or in the snow, the heart prints crisscrossing our land, arteries to the wildness of our woods, revealing paths I had never seen.

Footprint,
or We All Have Big Feet

My footprint, by comparison to the average American, is actually small. But that doesn't make it right, because really, in contrast with the rest of the world's population, my footprint, like most of us in this country, is too big— far too big.

This footprint I'm talking about is an ecological footprint, a concept designed by Redefining Progress, an organization based in Oakland working to make our economy and public policy sustainable. One method for doing this is by creating tools to measure and compare people's use of our earth's resources. As their Web site, http://myfootprint.org, states: "The ecological footprint [concept] measures how much land and water we need to produce the resources we consume and absorb the waste we make." They ask you to answer approximately fifteen questions, categorized under such headings as food, housing, and transportation, and then tabulate your answers so that you can "compare your ecological footprint to what other people use and to what is available on this planet."

Overall, my final score came to fourteen, which means, to sustain my current lifestyle, I'm dependent on the productive capacity of fourteen acres of the earth. The average United States citizen requires twenty-four acres, so my score falls well below that figure, but not low enough. Worldwide, only four and a half biologically productive acres exist per person; if everyone lived as I do, we would need three earths to sustain us. Mars and Venus aren't the answers.

I know that transportation is an Achilles' heel for me in this footprint idea. I travel roughly fifteen thousand miles per year, most of that in a long 110-mile commute. Sarah, on the other hand, only commutes eighteen miles per day, or roughly five thousand miles per year, and her car, though ten years older, gets twice as good fuel mileage. (I know, I should be driving the older car, but that's a different story.) So with the same answers on the quiz except for these two differences on transportation, Sarah scored a nine, meaning she only needs nine acres to sustain her lifestyle. Again, this is far below our national average and far above any global comparison. If we all lived at her rate, we would still need two earths to sustain us. Congress has yet to enact any policy to begin construction of another planet, and heaven help us if they do.

As with all such "quizzes," I had trouble fitting into their multiple-choice answers, but that's as much about my oddball-ality as anything else. The first question, for example, asks how much meat you eat, and I know the motive behind this is to demonstrate the horrendous use of energy put into our food supply. I do eat meat regularly, but almost all of it is venison that I hunt here on our farm. This, in turn, causes extremely little ecological damage and probably some ecological benefit, given the current deer overpopulation. So I had trouble with that question and some of the others that seemed to show the whole geared toward urban dwellers and not rural. But these quibbles are minor.

To take the concept to the extreme, I played with the quiz, punching in several of the most ecologically-conservative answers. If, for example, we were all vegans, grew our own food, lived in houses under a thousand square feet in size, never flew, stayed at home or walked or carpooled in vehicles that got over fifty miles per gallon, we would need five acres to survive. Given that there are over six billion people on our one little planet, this figure is close to the four-and-a-half target and thus close enough to sustainable.

I plan on growing a giant garden this year, but I'm not sure about riding my bicycle the fifty-five miles to work. But still, if we want to give our children and their children a healthy place to live, we need to change our ways. Take this quiz, and discover the changes we each need to make.

For the Love of Chicken

Whenever my neighbor and I talk religion, he always asks if I like chicken. John knows I grew up in the Methodist tradition, and along with his belief in God, he also believes that all Methodists love chicken. I'm guessing he's right; most Methodists I know do love to eat this bird, including myself.

But for years I avoided eating chicken. As a teen, I worked in a neighbor's chicken house. Once a year, a hundred people hired on to pull the sixty thousand chickens—called "layers"—out of their small cages in this building longer than a football field. Eight to ten birds at a time, we grabbed them by the legs and carried them squawking upside down to the Campbell's truck waiting to take them to a soup factory. In the cages, some of the birds' claws had grown around the wire floor. We had to break their legs to free them.

A week later, after the farmer cleaned out the manure pit and disinfected the house, we all came back to stuff sixty thousand new birds into cramped quarters, nine birds to a cage, a one-year sentence of no daylight or fresh air, no scratching of the earth, no grubs or bugs, just conveyor-belt food.

I avoided eggs and meat for years after this. I knew the life history of every grocery store egg and leg. But recently, I've rediscovered my love for this food, and I've found local farmers who raise their birds in a more humane way that's better for the bird, the land, and all of us.

For eggs, many area farmers still keep a small flock of layers. Instead of sixty thousand birds, each given a square foot of caged space, these small flocks of thirty or so get to see the sun every morning, roam the chicken yard every day, scratch the dirt as only chickens do, and roost quietly at night, clucking each other to sleep. I don't have a tongue good enough to taste the difference between these and store-bought eggs, but I know a healthier, happier bird makes for a healthier, happier me.

Some of these farmers are part of an international movement started in Virginia by Joel Salatin, a process of raising meat he calls Pastured Poultry. Again, instead of huge houses that confine a mass of birds into a small area, this method encourages a healthier animal by more closely following its natural life cycle. When the chickens become old enough to forage, the farmer moves them to a pasture where they live in moveable pens. Once a day, the farmer rolls the ten-by-ten-by-two-foot pen to a new spot where the birds have a grand time scratching and eating grass and bugs, which make up about 30 percent of their diet.

The system works better than the industrialized chicken factories because pastured poultry have access to sunlight and higher-quality food that is clean of steroids and antibiotics. This system also works more sustainably because the birds' waste is naturally spread over the field, tremendously improving its health as well. Farmers like this method because they save on food, fuel, and fertilizer costs, and they sell directly to the consumer, only growing as many birds as have been ordered; so far, the demand has far outpaced the availability. After seven to eight weeks, the farmers butcher the birds and the consumers pick them up on the very day they are butchered, guaranteeing freshness.

Pastured poultry also applies to turkeys. Farmers have a flock of the big birds in movable pens, receiving the same healthy treatment. The taste of these Thanksgiving birds is excellent and the demand high. Farmers have also experimented with pastured pigs as well as pastured layers, chickens in moveable shelters called Egg Mobiles or Egg Expresses. Again, all of the same benefits occur for these animals.

I've eaten several chickens raised this way and have savored their good taste and tenderness. They've also proved, once again, my neighbor's dictum about Methodists. Later this month, we'll pick up our order of eight birds.

The Holy, Lowly Spud

We grub for orbs of light: Kennebec, Pontiac, Yukon
Gold. Earth eggs perfect in their potato-ness. I kneel and
fork the soft ground, the smell rich of dry leaves and
black soil. Sarah watches each turn of earth, waits for me
to pause, then cradles the tan skins in her arm. She rubs
off dirt and settles each nugget into the bucket. We work
down the rows of dead plants this way, the bats darting
overhead for gnats.

We examine each potato, predicting futures: "home
fries," for a warty one; "a mountain of mashed," for the
next. We are treasure hunting for the next meal, the next
surprise. Sometimes we'll uncover a nose-shaped potato,
sometimes a thumb, body parts of a corpse turned tuber,
now growing in different parts of the garden.

The dogs join in the digging, paw where we're heading, snort in a mole hole for their own next meal. Becca,
our pup, even uncovers a potato and prances with it in
her mouth, flicking her tail, dancing around the garden
with her "look at me, look at me" grin. We toss her
another, watch her pounce.

I rest and recount for Sarah the potato patches of my
childhood. The whole clan gathered in the spring and fall

to work the ground of the family farm. Dad drove the red Cub tractor while I tried to lay off straight rows with an old horse plow, my uncles watching and teasing me for the crooked rows. Grandma and Grandpa had spent the day cutting the tubers into chunks, an eye or two per seed, a sprout to search for the vision of light. Then we cousins dropped each spud in its row while Dad and his brothers covered the rows with the tractor and old plow. In fall we hauled out that plow and cranked the Cub, and everyone filled their buckets. We harvested bushels enough to fill the root cellar, a food bank to draw from through the long winter.

Once on a visit home, my great-aunt Esther told me stories about my great-grandparents and potatoes, stories I'd never heard. They grew ten acres of spuds, *ten acres*, all with horse and plow. In this huge patch, Aunt Esther remembered picking the orange-striped potato beetles off the plants and dropping them into a mason jar of gasoline. The neighbors helped harvest the crop, singing and joking to ease the back-bending labor. Sometimes the bending over revealed spuds the size of two fists, spuds that filled sacks emptied into crates and stored in the cavern-like root cellar under the house, two hundred bushels a year. One year, they harvested so many potatoes that they had to store them on the barn floor where half of them froze before my great-grandfather could peddle them all in town.

Here in Virginia, Sarah and I don't peddle any potatoes; we only grow seven or eight bushels, enough to fill a side of the root cellar, enough to get us through the winter. Every year we work down each row of dying plants, work down the dusk of day, work down winter crate by crate.

Claiming Ground

Every cranny and nook of this root cellar gives voice to the elements. Moisture condenses on walls, makes the air thick with life, and the earth itself becomes more tangible here, holds all, gently. The dirt floor and rock walls connect me to an age older than memory. Though not readily apparent, the sun also inhabits this space. In the low ceiling, the joists speak of each season the trees grew towards the sun, their rings now translated into knots and lines. The bushels of potatoes on the floor, the buckets full of carrots packed in sawdust, the shelves lined with row upon row of jars—beans, beets, jams and jellies, pickles and peaches—talk their own tongue of sun, rain, earth, and air, just as we all do.

I enter the cellar to fetch some potatoes. When I rest my palm on the shale wall, I am immediately quieted by the room's abundant reserve and its cool, damp breath.

All over our farm, shale rises in solid, slanted veins. I've hauled plenty of this, the land's first crop, and know well the plate-sized, brittle-edged heft of stone. The builders of this homestead, Ira and Dellie Lester, probably found more shale bleeding from these veins than they wanted, yet they transformed the surplus into rock walls. One parallels the road, preventing hostas and daylilies from spilling into car tracks. Another dry wall acts as part of our house's foundation, preventing the two-story structure from sliding down the hill.

Behind the house, sharing a dogtrot roof, sits the source and prime user of this crop of rocks, the root cellar. Ira dug this ten-by-eight-by-six-foot hole, prying loose the slate with shovel, pick, and pry bar. If he found the right angle of vein, the shale fell away easily, and he saved the chunks to build the walls. If he hit bedrock, solid and dense, like at the back of the cellar, he had to chip loose each small chunk, sending it flying, sometimes into his eyes.

His work stood worn, solid but unused, when we bought the farm in the winter of 1991. By the next fall, the root cellar regained its name, and for five years, we stored our food and seeds there, the humid darkness sheltering sustenance for the long winter.

Every fall we dug potatoes, forking black richness in search of white. After kneeling for hours grubbing, we hauled the heavy crates uphill to the cellar, the sun touching these nuggets only briefly in their journey from darkness to darkness. I wondered often about Ira, the man who a hundred years ago planted potatoes in this garden, the man who now rode in his own narrow hole. As he dug this cavity, did he contemplate death? When he built the walls to keep the cold out, the life in, did he wonder how long this cellar would hold winter food, or who might use it after him? Did he wonder all of this or just swing the pick with the steady thought of finishing the job and eating supper?

Whatever his thoughts, the cellar outlasted him by forty years before it felt the cool hand of death—a wet death in this case. By 1996, the back wall bowed dangerously as water seeped behind it, freezing and thawing the dirt, displacing rock and mortar. Gravity worked slowly but with steady power. Rocks slid back into the hole, and Ira's mortar dissolved into dust and sand. I braced the ceiling to save the roof, and finally the whole wall collapsed. The loose rocks and dirt I pulled out piled higher, yet I had no idea how I would rebuild. With sunlight pouring in where a wall used to exist, I paused, for two years, to figure out the next step.

During this pause, I consulted everyone I knew who had any experience with concrete. At a reunion, my friendly questions turned into a family debate as my dad and three uncles argued over whether I should pour a concrete wall or build it with blocks. In the end, they all agreed that I should just burn it and start over.

Eventually, with sound advice from my brother-in-law, Paul, I decided to use block. I didn't have Ira's ingenuity, but I did have Paul, a carpenter/contractor who regularly built mansions in Charlotte. He agreed to help rebuild the cellar and arrived late one evening in January. The next day, we cleaned out more rock and dirt, hauled in cinder blocks, and set to work, me mixing mortar, Paul laying block. Even though he claimed not to be an expert, he deftly slapped the mortar in place and showed great creativity. In two places, he had to join the block wall with the existing stone one. This joint of square blocks with odd-shaped shale, the new thrust against the old, "gives 'ugly' a new definition," to use Paul's words. Yet, it worked.

We repeated this pattern of work the next day, except we kept on into the night and through a snow-storm. In the cellar, Paul laid block with the electric heater keeping him and the mortar warm. Outside, I mixed mortar and hauled in more blocks, trying to keep up with his quick pace. We finished the last row at 11:00 that night, with four inches of new snow muffling all sound. He left the next morning, having given us a grand start on the cellar. I had looked at this wall-less room for two years, and now to enter an enclosed space gave me needed hope.

Six months later, the whole Dowdey clan—Sarah's parents, Carl and Jerry, and Paul and his family—came for a visit to help again. Shortly after they arrived, we jacked up the building and slid into place two ceiling joists, heavy oak two-by-eights. Then we jacked up the hundred-year-old structure one last time, raising it over an inch and making it groan. With a sledgehammer, I tapped into place the six-by-six-inch locust sill, specially cut from our forest. Lastly, we fixed the door. Its hinge side had wiggled from the wall because no bottom sill held it firm. We slid in a two-by-eight and trimmed the door to make it shut tightly.

Through this whole process, both Carl and Paul asked why we would bother rebuilding something so old, run-down, and in many ways, poorly built. I responded briefly with something like, "We need to store our potatoes," or, "All the history here needs preservation." Both answers got at the reason. We *did* need a functional place to store our winter roots, and I did like the history of this building—the image of Ira seeing a cellar here, chipping out a hole one pick stroke at a time, then using this shale for walls and building a shed on top—all of it worth holding on to. But also, I wanted to rebuild this cellar to add my own history to this place, my own voice. I wanted this homestead to claim me as much as I had claimed it.

Later, after that weekend, I dug a trench behind the cellar to direct the water away from the building. On the clapboard siding, I discovered one of the many marks left by Ira and Dellie's son, W. Guy Lester. At the age of sixteen, he stood for an hour or so behind this shed, out of view of all; had he committed a wrong, or was he just entertaining himself during the dry Depression years? He carved into the boards, "W. G. L. June 6 1934," scrolled with caps on the letters and the day's date neatly tucked between the month and year. Though probably not yet born when his father built this structure, Guy had autographed it just the same.

In the same spirit, on the doorstep that Carl meticulously smoothed with fresh concrete, I scratched his and my initials along with Paul's and Sarah's and the year "1998" for whoever would come along a century after us, hoping that they, too, would preserve and use this cellar.

Finally, three years after the cellar caved in, sixty-five years after W. G. L. initialed it, and a hundred years after its creation, I finish the repairs. With the last of the insulation tacked into place, I sit on the cool ground and rest. So far the temperature has stayed around seventy degrees, even with ninety-five-degree days outside. But I know the insulation will eventually keep the temperature between thirty-five and fifty.

I want to check one last time for any cracks. I turn off the lightbulb and pull the door shut. Total darkness consumes me, so total that even after my eyes adjust, I can see nothing.

So this is what it'll be like, an opening into the earth, both a grave and a womb.

Corn Mazes

For me as a child, cornfields became massive hide-n-seek playgrounds. My friends and I bolted between rows with the rough leaves rubbing raw our cheeks and arms.

I ran through those same fields still later, as a teen with my best friend, Joe. Those miles of cornstalks became Halloween hideouts for our silly pranks. We would shell the hard corn with our hands, sneak to the edge where field met road, wait in the dark for piercing headlights, and then swing our handfuls of kernels out onto the car. The clatter of yellow "sleet" surprised the driver who usually stopped. And off we tore in separate directions through the maze, the moonlight barely giving us enough light to stay in the rows. Once the motorist moved on, it took us a half hour to find each other again.

On our farm, the corn itself was always a part of our lives. As a child, I helped at harvest time by riding the empty wagons to the field where I hooked and unhooked an empty for a full one. Then on the return trip I rode on top fifteen feet in the air, the massive pile of hard cobs and kernels against my back, the branches of cherry and willow brushing my cheek. I loved those rides.

In our daily farm chores when we fed the milk cows, flecks of chopped, yellow kernels sifted through our hands. And in our own diet, we supped on canned, frozen, creamed, and dried corn. My favorite was our annual summer ritual of roasting the sweet corn over a pit of coals. That mix of smoky sweetness makes my mouth water even now.

I've moved away from all of that, living hundreds of miles from family, farm, and those old rituals. Still, when the raccoons allow, I can grow a small patch of sweet corn for our own freezer and table. And lately, when city relatives visit, we've started a new ritual, visiting a maize maze.

Clay and Allison, my nephew and niece, have as much energy as can be packed into five- and nine-year-olds. On their recent visit, Allison ran up our steep, quarter-mile driveway four times just to set a world record, and Clay log-rolled for hours down the hill in front of our house. They wore us out in the first two hours of their visit.

To try to wear them out, we decided on a trip to the Williamses' orchard and corn maze, outside of Wytheville. For a small price, we rode in a hay wagon and wandered in a pumpkin patch, picking out the biggest and prettiest. We also got lost in their cannon-shaped corn maze. Mrs. Williams, the co-owner and an elementary school teacher, told us ahead of time that the ten stations within the maze all had questions tied to the state's Standards of Learning for third- and fourth-graders. Sarah, an elementary school teacher, was sworn to silence so the rest of us could answer the questions. Without her help, I found I needed to go back to third grade. I didn't know how many presidents hailed from Virginia (eight), how many counties lie within its borders (ninety-six, if I remember right), or, what I thought an easy one, how many geographic regions it has (four).

Luckily the questions were all multiple choice, and we chose path A, B, or C, depending on our guess. If we guessed incorrectly, we either circled back to the station or found ourselves at a dead end. With Allison and Clay plunging ahead, we ran through those towering plants. The constant rub of rough leaves on face and arms brought back all those memories of hide-and-seek and corn marauding. But I couldn't reminisce long; I had to huff it to keep up with the kids. Even with a few false turns, we finished the puzzle in record time, wishing it was twice as long.

We exited the nine-acre maize maze into one of the Williamses' orchards, and at the top of a hill, we came to the grand finale. Two young men, kin to the Williams clan, had constructed a real pumpkin cannon by welding a long pipe and a used water tank onto the back of a dump truck. Our hosts would put a large volume of air pressure into the tank, roll a small pumpkin down the cannon's barrel, raise the dump truck bed to the right angle, and every half hour, with a crowd of onlookers, release the pressure and watch the orange cannonball fly. In less than a few seconds, the missile arched over grazing heifers to land in an alfalfa field 650 yards away. A little ingenuity for a whole lot of amusement.

Throughout the country, corn mazes have become more and more common, giving everyone the chance to feel the rough rub of these amazing plants. Visit one and get lost. The kids will sleep all the way home.

Cussed Yellow Jackets

The past summer, like the many summers before, I mowed the yard too many times. And again this past summer, like the many summers before, I mowed over some small hole in the ground, a hole that I didn't know existed, a hole full of yellow jackets.

Now, I know what to do—forget the mower and run. Still I usually get stung four or five times as I dash to the house. The first summer, though, I didn't know what bulleted my legs or where these shots came from. Before I understood to look down and run, I ended with ballooned legs and too many stings to count. I cussed a lot, too.

But the yellow jackets have their own language. Even if they could understand my swearing, they would just laugh; what good is a cuss word when you have a stinger? A basic primary to yellow jacket language goes something like this: create a nest, either in the eaves of a house or in a mole hole in the ground; lay as many eggs as you can; attack any creature that threatens you or your nest, especially the tall ones who push a noisy, worthless machine around the yard; and keep attacking. Unlike honeybees that disembowel themselves when

they sting, and then die, yellow jackets can sting repeatedly and live on. They seem to relish this ability.

What to do when these creatures hole up in your
yard? Unfortunately not much can be done. I've tried the
various sprays, reluctantly, and with little success.
Usually I either mow over them with the riding (not push)
lawn mower in high gear, or just avoid that spot.

But there is one technique that I've seen actually
work well—skunks. These striped creatures feast on yellow jackets and their eggs, and somehow, they don't
seem to mind the stings. I've witnessed several full nests
dug out of the ground. Overnight the cavities of baby
bombers are completely destroyed. The trick is to invite
the skunk without getting yourself or your pets sprayed.
I've read of putting out a molasses-and-grain mixture
right beside a yellow jacket hole, but have never tried it.
I know my dogs would find it first and come back with
molasses dripping from their lips and yellow jackets
clinging to their noses.

My father-in-law, though, has tried just about every
trick, including some he invented himself. A patient man,
Carl is a retired engineer who reads car manuals in his
spare time. He enjoys figuring things out.

Like me, Carl also got stung last summer while mowing his backyard. He is more allergic to the stings,

though, and one time his granddaughter came screaming from the swing set followed by an angry swarm. He knew he had to do something, so he set to destroying the nest he found in the ground. He knows persistence, but so do these creatures. First he used a twenty-foot pole to jab into the ground. He wanted to crush and ruin that nest, but that didn't work. He tried shoveling out the swarm, repeatedly taking a scoop of dirt and running. That didn't work either. Next he shoveled a huge pile of dirt on top of the nest and tamped it down solid. They dug through and kept multiplying, and stinging.

When he mowed, he pushed the mower across the nest and then ran to the other side to get it. One time he started the mower and just parked it over the nest, leaving it there for an hour till it ran out of gas. It only made the yellow jackets angrier.

Carl then resorted to poisons. He tried the several different sprays on the market, with no effect. He became more desperate, more obsessed, less concerned with the health of his yard, so he poured used motor oil into the hole, to no avail, then old paint. The yellow jackets now were blue, and he saw them down the street boasting to each other about their new coats. Finally, he disobeyed the city ordinances where he lives and built a fire on top of the nest, dousing the flames with plenty of kerosene.

What finally got rid of them? "Persistence," he said, "just a whole lot of persistence." He didn't think any one technique completely worked.

The next time, though, he wants to try filling the holes with sand, or better yet, spraying with a fire extinguisher.

Shocked

When we were quite small, my cousin and I would go behind the barn and see who could pee the farthest. One day his older brother discovered us and dared us to pee over the electric fence. We never played that game again.

Recently, I've come back "in touch" with electric fencing, this time as a way to save our orchard from deer. Like the Cherokee who have always valued and loved deer, I too have come to respect the deer, felt its nourishment in my body, and admired its white tail waving farewell. Historically, deer have provided food for both the body and the eye.

But like most farmers and gardeners, I've also felt anger and frustration at these animals, especially when they chewed off the tops of our young orchard. We planted eighteen trees two years ago and surrounded each seedling with a four-foot, plastic tree tube. I had hoped foolishly that these tubes would protect them, but soon learned that the deer destroyed each limb as quickly as it poked out of the tube. I began to understand my neighbor's hatred, a hatred that made the deer the mammalian equivalent to the cockroach—prolific, voracious, and stubbornly persistent.

A simple, single-strand electric fence saved our orchard, for a while anyway. I had read about several different types of fences and even saw, in central Virginia, an elaborate, twelve-foot monster that guarded a two-acre orchard, all for the price of $10,000. I had neither the time nor money for such, but I did have another option. The deer hadn't made our orchard into a permanent bedding area yet, so I thought this method might work. Called the Minnesota Single-Strand Electric Fence, it made my neighbors laugh in disbelief when they heard about it, especially when I told them of the bait.

Ignoring their laughter, I borrowed my neighbor's fence post auger, dug corner postholes, then went to work setting locust posts in these corners. Between the posts, every twenty-five feet or so, I drove a four-foot stake. I used cheap rebar for these middle stakes and bought special insulators that fit over rebar and work well. I stretched the twenty-gauge wire from post to post, connected the wire to the charger and the charger to a copper grounding rod. This charger, or "juicer," sends a pulse of electricity through the whole system once every other second, a jolt strong enough to make me jump, even when I'm expecting it.

The fence's simplicity makes it both laughable and beautiful. The single wire, for best results, is two to three feet off the ground. The deer can easily jump it but don't because we entice them to touch the fence with one of our own favorite foods: peanut butter.

Once I had the fence ready, Sarah and I worked on the bait. She wrapped strips of foil around the wire every ten feet, and I smeared a peanut-butter/vegetable-oil mixture on the strips and on the wire itself. The foil works to make sure the deer see the wire, and the peanut butter makes sure they touch it.

Though not as fool-proof as the $10,000 model, this fence has easily covered its costs. The locust posts came from the farm, and the charger, wire, insulators, and rebar totaled around $200, the charger being the largest expense. The deer have broken the fence three times in the initial two years—two of those times after I had expanded the boundary—but all three times, they did no damage to the trees. I'd guess they were so startled by the jolt that they turned right around without even sniffing the apples.

For more information on fences and pest control, see the Appendix beginning on page 267.

We Create the World We Eat:
The Benefits of Organic Food

In the freshman writing courses I teach, I ask students to read and write about food. We "digest" *Fast Food Nation*, Eric Schlosser's best-seller aptly subtitled "The Dark Side of the All-American Meal." After Schlosser describes the slaughterhouse practices and the many diseases that taint our food, students often look anew at what they eat. Some even become vegetarians or give up fast food, as one did, for Lent.

Then I ask students to explore any aspect of food, and they research subjects from what farmers feed cattle to what athletes should eat for optimum performance. I usually learn from them as they uncover new sources, but this past semester one student's paper especially educated me. Elizabeth Manning's topic, "Why We All Should Eat Organic," covered the environmental and economical aspects of these farming practices, information I already knew for the most part. But then she researched the health aspects of eating organic, and a scientific study she found is worth sharing.

A 1993 study published in the *Journal of Applied Nutrition* by Bob L. Smith compared the mineral content of organic produce with conventionally grown. Over a two-year period in Chicago, Smith bought apples, pears, potatoes, wheat, and corn of both categories, and analyzed them in his lab. He discovered a significant nutrient difference in favor of organic produce. The organic corn, for example, had 1,600 percent more manganese, 1,800 percent more calcium, and 2,200 percent more iodine than regular corn. On average, organic produce had two and one-half times more nutrients than conventionally grown, primarily due to the health of the soil and type of fertilizer. Smith noted that many studies, including a surgeon general's, "have found that low levels of elements correlate with many health conditions," from "alcoholism, allergy, [and] cancer," to "chronic fatigue . . . , diabetes . . . , and rheumatoid arthritis." Smith concluded, "The elements found to reduce symptoms are the same elements found in this study at greater concentration in organic food."

On the Organic Trade Association's Web site, a more recent study confirms this older one. In 2001, Virginia Worthington, of Johns Hopkins University, reviewed "forty-one published studies comparing the nutritional value of organically grown and conventionally grown" foods. She found significant differences of several major nutrients. Overall, Worthington showed that organic crops have "27% more vitamin C, 21.1% more iron, [and] 29.3% of magnesium." The organic produce also had "15.1% less nitrates," the residues left from fertilizers and pesticides. Depending on how it's grown, the proverbial apple a day could help you a lot or not at all.

Curious to find more research on the benefits of organic produce, I discovered several other studies. One from *New Scientist*, published in 2002, documents a British study of salicylic acid in organic soups. This acid, a plant-produced defense mechanism, acts in our bodies as an anti-inflammatory that also combats bowel cancer and artery hardening. The British scientists reveal that organic vegetable soup has on average almost nine times more salicylic acid than regular, non-organic soups. As a result, "eating organic food may help reduce your risk of heart attacks, strokes, and cancer."

The population most affected by this debate over how crops are grown are those with no voice—our children. In 2002, a research team headed by Cynthia Curl at the University of Washington proved that children who eat an organic diet are exposed to far fewer pesticides. Their study, published in *Environmental Health Perspectives*, focused on two groups of preschoolers, assessing diets and urine samples. The twenty-one children who ate conventionally grown food had a concentration of a certain pesticide *nine times higher* than the eighteen children who ate primarily organic food. This high level of toxin exceeded the Environmental Protection Agency's recommendations. As the authors conclude, "Consumption of organic produce appears to provide a relatively simple way for parents to reduce their [children's] exposure to . . . pesticides."

Whether we realize it or not, eating is a political and environmental act. Each bite affects our health as well as that of all creatures, from the soil microorganism to the farmer. Granted, organic food usually costs more than conventionally grown, but what is the true cost of health? As Barbara Kingsolver writes, "Before anyone rules out eating . . . organically because it seems expensive, I'd ask [them] to figure in the costs paid *outside* the store: the health costs, the land costs, the big environmental Visa bill that sooner or later comes due."

We can work to improve the health of our planet and our own bodies by eating and growing organic food, or we can improve the wallets of doctors and agribusiness CEOs while sending tons of soil and pesticides downriver every day.

Everytime we take a bite, we create the same world that we eat.

If you would like to know more about organic food, a useful list of resources can be found in the Appendix beginning on page 267.

Beyond Organic

Imagine you're standing in the produce section of your local grocery faced with a variety of apples. You want to make the best choice, for the good of your family, farm workers, and the environment. Do you buy the organic Galas shipped from across the country or the Granny Smiths grown conventionally but locally?

The decision is not easy.

First, consider organic. Organic farming, because it shuns synthetic fertilizers and pesticides, is friendlier to the environment than conventional practices. And evidence published in many reputable journals increasingly illustrates that organic food is better for you. No wonder consumers have made organic food the fastest-growing sector of agriculture with sales of organic food rising by 20 percent annually.

But organic is not without problems. As these sales have grown, organic farming has moved away from its small, family-farm roots and is becoming industrialized. The organic carrots I buy at Wal-Mart were probably grown on a large scale, a system dependent on fossil-fuel mechanization, underpaid farm labor, and imported organic fertilizers. How sustainable over the long run is the diesel tractor plowing up the soil? How fair are the labor practices? And the chicken-litter fertilizer might be organic, but how far was it shipped before it was spread on the field?

This distance question highlights a problem of our entire food system, including organic: our love affair with airlifted, railroaded, tractor-trailored grapes in December or tomatoes in February. Often this produce comes from Mexico or Chile or some other faraway place, and its cheap price belies the waste of energy used to transport it to our tables.

"Eaters might begin to question the sanity of eating food more traveled than they are," quips Joan Dye Gussow, author of *This Organic Life*. Noting that a calorie is a unit of energy, she says, "It costs 435 fossil fuel calories to fly a 5-calorie strawberry from California to New York."

This burning of fossil fuel to move food means more globe-warming greenhouse gases. My organic carrots from Wal-Mart might do my body good, but in eating them, I'm harming the larger body of our earth, and that ultimately circles back to everyone's health.

Now consider locally grown food. It solves the problem of shipping food long distances. The Granny Smith from your nearby orchard only has to travel a few miles, in contrast with the one to two thousand miles that most of our food travels from field to plate. Because of this short commute, local food—organic or conventional—is naturally fresher and tastier.

Another advantage of buying locally is food security. Today's centralized system processes food in huge factories and moves products in large quantities, creating attractive targets for terrorists looking to contaminate as much food as possible. A decentralized system of small, local farms and processors would be much harder to disrupt.

That fresh produce packs one more punch; it allows you to know your community. You and your family begin to understand where your food comes from, maybe even meeting the farmer. If this grower doesn't use organic methods, you can ask him to try. Seek out a local farmers' market or vegetable subscription service that provides a weekly bag of produce, and find the small growers who don't have to exploit labor to gather their harvests.

So next time you are in the supermarket pondering the organic Gala or the local Granny Smith, consider how you might create a food system that is both organic and local. If you enjoy quality food and a healthy planet, analyze what you eat; where was it grown and how? The ultimate way to have both local and organic is to plant and harvest your own food, even if it is just a few tomato plants or one apple tree. Even if you live in a city or cold climate, fresh lettuce, organic *and* local, can be had, even in January.

Learn more about fresh organic produce from the resources in the Appendix beginning on page 267.

Star Linked

Consider this: Depending on the poll, anywhere from 80 to 95 percent of Americans want genetically engineered (GE) foods to be clearly labeled and tested for safety. The vast majority of us don't want GE corn contaminating our taco shells, whether it is the unapproved StarLink variety or a particular GE corn "approved" for human consumption. Despite popular sentiment, though, roughly 60 percent of grocery store and restaurant food contains unlabeled ingredients derived from genetically modified crops or other organisms. And despite the growing public demand, the Food and Drug Administration issued its proposed federal regulation on GE foods, refusing to call for mandatory testing or labeling. Something is amiss.

Scientists create a biotech crop by inserting genetic material from a different organism into a particular plant's genes, introducing a new desired trait. For example, Monsanto creates Roundup-Ready soybeans, plants that survive the company's Roundup herbicide. This allows farmers to spray their fields and kill weeds but not the crop. Another GE plant is Bt corn, designed to produce a natural pesticide that kills the European corn borer. This supposedly allows the farmer to use less pesticide.

But in many ways, it seems, we are blundering into the unknown. The benefits of GE plants are short-lived—weeds and pests adapt and develop resistance just as they do to other herbicides and pesticides. And we don't know what these new organisms will do to the environment. What will be the long-term results? Drifting pollen has already contaminated other crops throughout the Midwest, and "super pests," like cotton boll worms in China, are developing resistance to Bt cotton. Unlike Bt sprays used by organic growers, Bt crops exude the toxin into the soil in substantial quantities where it lasts up to eight months, possibly affecting essential soil organisms in adverse ways. The short-term benefits are steadily being exhausted around the world.

Likewise, we don't know what GE crops and their foreign proteins do to humans. Our ignorance is underscored by the fact that there has been almost no peer-reviewed scientific research published that proves GE crops are safe. Our environment and our bodies have become guinea pigs for morally impoverished companies bent on monetary wealth.

People from all nationalities realize that food is sacred. Native Americans took thousands of years to breed and develop corn, and plant breeders have continued this traditional work in recent history, most notably

Nobel Prize-winner Barbara McClintock. If only all of us could see corn's sacredness, we wouldn't be modifying its very genes and then calling it StarLink. Corn is already linked to the stars, as are we all.

For a list of publications about genetically engineered foods, visit the Appendix beginning on page 267.

Not Ready
for Roundup's Results

Tony and Mary operate a small farm in southwest
Virginia. Like many, they moved to the country for a better life, and to finance this, they turned to growing
grapes. Over the past decade, they've planted and tended a small vineyard and recently began making their
own wine. I've picked those grapes, tasted their sweetness, and relished the full flavor of Mary and Tony's
kindness; they are good friends.

But the better life turned bitter recently when Mary
was diagnosed with non-Hodgkin's lymphoma (NHL), a
form of cancer. The taste of the diagnosis turned even
more sour when they learned the probable cause: the
herbicide Roundup that they regularly used on their
farm. I can only imagine Tony's anger and pain at this
realization. I know he handled the poison with caution,
wore safety equipment, and sprayed only on windless
days and never around the house. He followed the directions on the label, but maybe they were wrong, and this
puts everyone at risk.

Though Tony and Mary have no direct proof that
Roundup caused Mary's cancer, scientists have begun to

question the herbicide's marketed innocence. In 1999, Roundup's active ingredient, glyphosate, was linked to non-Hodgkin's lymphoma. Swedish scientists Drs. Lennart Hardell and Mikael Eriksson published their study in the *Journal of the American Cancer Society*, finding that exposure to glyphosate "yielded increased risks for NHL." The report has since been criticized for relying too much on case studies, and no one has yet conducted a double-blind study of glyphosate. But the *Journal of Pesticide Reform* found over a hundred other studies all illustrating the lethal toxicity of this chemical.

Monsanto, Roundup's manufacturer, churns out this chemical at an incredible rate and markets it as one of the safest on the shelves. According to a *New York Times* report from August 2001, Monsanto "produces close to 160 million gallons a year," which makes Roundup "the best-selling agricultural chemical product ever, with $2.8 billion in sales" in 2000. It is an international success that "outsells other chemicals five to one."

Why so popular? Roundup effectively kills just about everything, and Monsanto markets it to just about everyone. Like a household cleaner, you can find it premixed in a spray bottle ready to use in any hardware store. My parents use it on dandelions in their yard, my neighbors use it to kill the thistle in their pastures, and other farmers spray millions of acres with it before they plant. It has become the mainstay of "no-till" agriculture, a method of farming that prevents soil erosion by substituting the spray gun for the plow, but at what cost? And with what kind of warnings?

Sadly, glyphosate is even more pervasive than most people realize because of genetically-modified seeds called "Roundup Ready." According to the *New York Times*, these seeds "account for almost 70 percent of the 70 million soybean acres [planted] in the United States." The plants tolerate the herbicide, which, as the USDA found in 1997, "resulted in a 72% increase in the use of glyphosate." Pushed to make more money, farmers spray up to three times more Roundup on these crops. The resultant poisonous residues have been found in wells, rainwater, and our food. Maybe this explains why, as the Leukemia and Lymphoma Society reports, the "incidence of NHL rose 80 percent from 1973 to 1997" and that roughly sixty-four thousand people will be diagnosed each year. All of us, through our daily bread, are exposed to glyphosate and its resulting, cancerous dangers.

Recently I visited the neighborhood Lowe's and read the shelf of Roundup labels. Tony told me that none of the labels mention cancer, just "moderate eye irritation." If dogs and other domestic animals ingest large amounts, the chemical could cause "temporary gastrointestinal irritation," but there is no mention of the dangers to humans. Labels on the higher concentrate warn to "wear personal protective equipment" such as "long sleeved shirts and long pants, shoes plus socks."

All of the labels confirmed Tony's reading. Not one mentioned cancer; not one acknowledged that the tests only analyzed oral ingestion, not the much more lethal inhalation; not one mentioned that the combination of chemicals in Roundup is more lethal than the individual ingredients; not one explained the long-term toxicity, the genetic damage, the effects on reproduction, or the carcinogenicity, all confirmed by scientists independent of corporate money; not one label mentioned any of this.

Mary is still battling the cancer. It continues to appear in other parts of her body. None of us will ever be ready for such results from Roundup. The FDA should require a clear warning of the potential for cancer and encourage independent scientific studies of glyphosate. Likewise, Monsanto should act responsibly to give accurate and adequate warnings on Roundup labels.

It is only fair that we are at least warned.

Zone

Only in sports is "zone" a good word. For the rest of us, especially in rural areas, "zone" has become a four-letter word because we feel it threatens our independence. "I want to do what I want to do on my own land because it *is* my own land." I've said this and have heard many others say it too.

But I question how long we'll keep thinking this. What if poorly planned subdivisions, or worse—incinerators, landfills, or other heavy polluters—move in and surround us? Such is the case, or has been the threat, in many Virginia counties in our region. We need to examine the lessons these places offer and apply them to where we live.

I've been helping my brother-in-law and his family look for land in several areas in our valley, and this search has opened my eyes.

In a neighboring county, we drove through one poorly planned subdivision after another. The land developers had built cheap roads and partitioned off as many lots as possible. The roads full of potholes would never match state requirements; the lots were poorly laid out, squeezing as many as possible into one area; and the number of septic tanks in such close quarters made me wonder about the water quality. I'm not against trailers or dou-blewides, but I am against actions that compromise the health of people, their land, and their future, all for greed. In the past year, this county's supervisors passed a zoning law that requires all future developments to meet stricter, saner guidelines. But did they wait too long to do this?

In another nearby county, we learned of a different set of problems with which their Board of Supervisors has already dealt: becoming a rural dumping ground for urban problems. In the past ten years, this county has fought off several large corporate interests that threat-ened the health of their land and communities. In 1990, a proposed medical incinerator was almost built, but enough people foresaw the health risks of what would come out of the smokestack that they fought the inciner-ator proposal all the way to the State Supreme Court. The Board of Supervisors, to prevent future similar prob-lems, passed zoning laws. And similar proposals did come, like a solid-waste landfill and a nuclear-waste dump, both of which were defeated because they would have degraded the land and people's health. Currently the citizens are fighting the power company's proposed 765kV power line. The years of fighting have shown that much of urban America sees its rural counterparts as a place to get rid of their problems, whether through high-security prisons, mega-landfills, or medical incinerators.

But as John Dodson, my friend in Bland County, Virginia, told me, "Zoning isn't always the answer. The answer is open, responsive government and an active, engaged, informed citizenry." And he is right. Our land and our own lives never have been and never will be fully independent. We all belong to communities, of other people, of plants, of animals, of the land itself. And most importantly, we have the responsibility to maintain and improve the health of those communities, including the health of the generations to come.

The Trouble with "Waste"

If nature had its own dictionary, "waste" would not be in it. No "waste" exists in that world—a fallen tree becomes a termite's home; and a cow patty in the pasture becomes a fly's birth ward, the grass's supper.

We humans do waste, though, as seen by the roadsides full of recyclable trash. We hear it in our clichés and songs, ("waste of time," "wasted away again in Margaritaville"), and most of us participate in it every time we turn on a light switch or start the car, our luxuries polluting our very necessities of air and water and soil. Anyone who visits the local nursing home bears witness to the "wasting" of human life itself.

This word, then, is a human construct derived from a human view of the world. Wendell Berry, in his classic *The Unsettling of America*, dissects this view well, articulating how we "waste" because we only live and think in a straight line, while the rest of the natural world lives in a circle. This straight line gives us concepts possible only in a human vocabulary, like industrial and hazardous wastes, hardwood pallets used only once, or pig factories and their huge mega-lagoons full of manure. Throughout the south, these lagoons are emptied onto the surrounding farms. Normally this spreading of manure replenishes the land, continues the circle, but at this horrific scale, the fields adjacent to these factories have become so over-saturated with nutrients that they have to be monitored for toxicity. A small, diversified farm would never have this problem.

What might this circle look like in our lives? A vegetable garden provides a good model. We expend our energy planting, hoeing, and harvesting the tomatoes, beans, and broccoli while the very food we cultivate replenishes that energy we spend.

So the model of the circle implies giving back and living within limits, of composting the leftover kitchen scraps and eating seasonally and from our local landscapes. We still have enough farmers and farmland left to create regional food systems, even in our most urbanized areas. What would it be like to know that the majority of our food came from within 250 miles of home versus half a world away? Imagine how much more healthful the food, how much less pollution, and how secure this food network would be, compared with today's system.

For such a vision to take place, we need to move beyond our current society's primary, linear goal of wealth and live in the circle's underlying value of health. As Berry notes, the word "health" shares the same roots as "holy," "heal," and "whole." To seek health means to seek wholeness, not just in our own lives, but in the whole, holy community that surrounds us, the whole community of flora and fauna that we depend upon and also need to begin healing, the whole community that doesn't know the meaning of "waste."

Working Among Trees

Sunlight on Willow

Late one evening while driving home, I round the last bend before our house and am greeted by sunlight on willow. Our small valley has filled with evening shadow, but the setting sun has flooded a side hollow with light, illuminating this single tree. The weeping willow still has its leaves, though yellowing and soon to fall. Each leaf in that last autumn light becomes a candle flicker, a spark igniting the whole tree.

We planted this weeping willow in 1995, and already I have to crane my neck to find the top while its curtain of branches brushes us with each passing. We dug the hole for this slip next to the huge, fallen trunk of another willow planted here by Ira and Dellie Lester in the early 1900s. In a scratched black-and-white photograph from the 1940s, the Lester homestead looks as it does today, a frame house overlooking the barn and small meadow. When I look out our wavy-glass windows, I see the same dirt road and silver maple that Ira stood beside sixty years ago. Trees cover the hills now instead of pasture, and the barn and house have tin roofs instead of wooden shingles. But at the bottom of the photo, beside Lost Bent Creek, the Lester willow tree shimmers in the same sun.

Ira and Dellie have long been buried, along with their two children, but their daughter-in-law still lives nearby. When I researched the history of this place, she kindly spent hours answering my questions and then loaned me her old photographs for me to copy. After one of our visits, she took me outside her house and showed off her small orchard and huge, well-tended garden. A weeping willow filled the center of the yard, its yellow wood peeking through thin leaves, its branches dancing with the wind. My friend told me to return in the spring, the best time to propagate willows, and she'd give me a cutting.

I did return several times, and when the weather was right, she gave me lopers, and I pruned off a one-inch-thick whip. That skinny stick now reaches twenty-five feet, and the trunk is at least a foot in diameter. A buck horned it two years ago, but the thick bark just healed over the wound.

From this mother tree, we've continued to take cuttings and plant more willows along Lost Bent Creek. We prune a suitable branch (anywhere from one to three inches in diameter), cut smaller whips from the branch, slice a foot-deep hole in the ground with a dibble or spade, slip in a whip, and tamp the ground around the stem. Willows love moisture and usually propagate easily along stream banks.

I'm guessing the Lester willow lived at least seventy-five years before a storm toppled it. Hopefully this young willow we planted will live as long, continuing to capture the sun's last light.

Hitting the Mark

I love splitting wood, especially *in* the woods. After having cut a log into rounds, I'll hike out a day or month later, carrying my maul, and split the pieces into chunks for the woodstove. The quiet of the woods envelopes me, especially in contrast to working with the chain saw. I can pause, and pause often to watch and listen.

Once several summers ago, I worked on the remains of a huge oak. As I split its top, a family of pileated woodpeckers came to inspect. Three youngsters, their red, pointed heads not fully developed, surrounded my small clearing, while mother worried over them from fifty feet away. They bobbed back and forth, listening for bugs under the bark, then peering down at me, "cack-cack-cacking" to each other. Then, as quickly as they came, they pumped the air and disappeared.

Recently, I've been getting home from work to hike out and split some maple and birch near our pond. I enjoy this last half hour of the daylight the most because I work out the kinks of spending too much time in an office. Instead of sitting at a computer, I use my whole body, stretch and feel its strength, actually "work out." All around, the world wakes or settles for the night. Last evening I glimpsed a great horned owl glide silently out of a pine grove and down the hollow, searching for its first meal of the night.

Not every time do I enjoy splitting wood, though, like when I get into a twisted locust or hickory full of knots, or worse, a black gum. I do all I can to avoid cutting gums and sycamores. Instead of a normal, clean split of an oak or maple, these trees form their rings differently, and when I try to split them, their lines zigzag into a wood-splitter's nightmare.

Usually I work with easier woods, like birch and oak, or one of the easiest, maple. I set the rounds on end and heave the eight-pound maul over my head. Then I swing the tool with all my might into the block of wood. As a teen, it took me a year or so to master the hardest part, hitting the mark, making a straight cut across the round instead of having the maul hit randomly.

Once I learned how to "aim" with the handle, I became entranced with the rhythm, whacking steadily, reaching my arms into the sky, riving open a piece of cherry, revealing for the first time its red inside.

Masonry Stoves

We heat with wood, and, for the most part, this affords us many pleasures. We get to stay in shape by cutting and carrying four to five cords of oak, locust, and maple every year. We improve our woodlot, felling the weak trees and making room for the healthier ones. And we save money on our power bill by keeping the electric heater turned off.

Burning wood, however, has its drawbacks. To avoid a creosote chimney fire, we clean the flue every year. Some people tire of the constant stoking of flame and sweeping of dirt. The main drawbacks for us, though, are the temperature fluctuations and extreme dryness. Even though we've heated with wood for over ten years, we still get the house too hot, which makes for miserable sleeping, or too cold, which makes for miserable waking up. Also, by January of every year, the inside of my nose feels like a desert lizard's skin. We run a humidifier, but its little spurt of steam seems futile.

Through research, I've found another type of stove that sounds like it solves many of these problems. Called a masonry stove, or sometimes a Russian or European stove, this method of heating with wood dates back centuries and is much older than the metal-box version we use today. While our iron-box, smoldering-style stove maintains a much higher temperature, the masonry stove's heat radiates from a mass of firebrick and tile. This eliminates much of the dryness and lessens the temperature fluctuations because the mass holds the heat and then gives it off slowly and steadily.

The tons of masonry also head off other problems. Because the smoke travels through a series of channels, it enters the chimney at a much cooler temperature. This reduces pollution and increases fuel efficiency (the wood's heat stays in the bricks rather than going up the chimney). Because the tile holds the heat so much more than our iron stove, the masonry stove only needs firing once or twice a day, eliminating the constant tending and the need to gather as much wood.

To verify what I read, I talked to Harry and Gail Groot, some friends who have been using a masonry stove for nearly a decade. They vouched for all of the benefits. They use half as much wood, enjoy the comfort of constant heat, don't have dry noses, and only fire the stove once a day (twice when it turns bitter cold). The only problem they've encountered is a crack in one of the exterior tiles, a surface fault, that isn't dangerous. Cracks are the most common problem because the intense heat makes the brick expand and contract, and masons have to allow room for this movement.

Harry's only regret is that he didn't isolate the firebox from the cast wall sections with a sheet of rock wool, or Nomex, a high-temperature insulation. This would keep the outside walls from getting so hot and popping tiles off. Otherwise, he's been happy with the masonry stove. He ended our interview by saying that 2001 will be their tenth year with it. Before that, they had twenty years of smoldering-fire, iron-box stove experience, and they wouldn't go back.

Praise for One Tough Tree

If you need to build a deck, fence, playground equipment, or any outdoor structure, consider the black locust. This native tree grows prolifically, providing the soil with nitrogen "fixed" from the air and offering the bees excellent nectar. It also provides us humans with high-quality firewood and some of the most durable lumber ever. The green-colored heartwood resists rot even when buried in the earth for decades. I've heard many farmers praise the tree's toughness and have helped put in enough fence posts to know these farmers speak the truth.

To verify their claims, I talked to Dr. Karl Polson, a friend who teaches natural resources management and agriculture at Pulaski High School. Karl, who is also a sawyer, confirmed that "we aren't using our natural resources," mainly the locust. Instead we import pine treated with chromated copper arsenic (CCA), two heavy metals and a poison that pose many environmental dangers. These hazards include leaching into the ground and water, and being taken up by plants, especially root crops. Additionally, when this lumber is burned, the smoke can and has killed people. Simply wiping a cloth over a piece of this wood picks up traces of arsenic, so imagine how much poison a child playing on a pressure-treated jungle gym absorbs. Avoid this unnatural, green wood and use locust instead. Besides, as Karl points out, "Good heartwood locust should equal or outlast any treated pine."

On our farm, we've used locust in several ways. Like many of our neighbors, we've used locust posts to fence our orchard. When we needed to replace a six-by-six-inch sill in our root cellar, we hired a sawyer with his band-saw mill to specially cut this beam. He also milled boards of other dimensions that we've used as steps, handrails, and the legs for our new picnic table. We plan for this wood to last a long time.

Using black locust also improves the local economy by investing in regional resources and people instead of giving money to the big suppliers that keep getting bigger. So use locust instead of pressure-treated lumber, and begin to appreciate this wood so tough that a friend calls it "organic cement."

The Slow Work of Healing

January 11, 1994—thirty-one degrees, and rain keeps falling in the New River Valley. Slowly the ice forms on roofs, roads, and trees, a horrifying beauty.

Even without electricity for five days, we are safe and warm with our woodstove. But the forest is not. The trees keep bending under this clear, clinking weight. Like Robert Frost, we know that "once they are bowed / So low for long, they never right themselves." The birches slowly stretch to the ground.

Within a month, a second ice storm of the same intensity covers the woods again. We sit in our house and listen to the branches pop like gunfire, trees killed by the buckshot of freezing raindrops.

Afterward, in the too-late sunshine, we venture into the clinking, dripping mess of woods. Birches arch over roads; limbless maples and pines poke the sky with splintered trunks. Other trees also feel the weight: huge poplars, oaks, and uprooted hemlocks. The destruction overwhelms us.

Most of this damage occurs on the side of one hill, in roughly seven acres. Five years earlier, Hurricane Hugo struck twenty poplars on the same hillside. These poplars live on, but the tops of each tree rest only five feet from the ground, instead of one hundred feet. With the hurricane poplars leaning uphill, the stripped pines upright, and the birches arching downhill, the area looks like an abandoned building—a roofless cathedral of broken glass.

We walk through this broken woods often, and year by year, we do the slow work of helping the forest repair itself, the slow work of healing. Those ice storms become valuable teachers by showing us the definition of a healthy tree: straight and upright; vigorous and solid; unforked and free of insects, diseases, and injuries. The county forester helps us create a map of what we have and where we want to go with our woods, a forest management plan. One of the primary tools of this is timber stand improvement (TSI).

I've practiced TSI acre by acre, winter by winter. Finally this year, I've finished that seven-acre hillside. The salvageable logs we sold or milled for our own use, and the rest we've let rot on the forest floor or burned as firewood. The black birch has warmed us many winters.

Dennis Anderson, the county forester, taught me the basics of TSI. "More than by species," he advised, "make your decisions based on form and health." Even if you want the high-value walnut, if it's forked or diseased, it should come out to make room for straighter saplings.

Also, by valuing form and health more than species, you'll end up with a greater diversity, which also improves the forest's health.

Section by section, I've picked out the best trees, the ones I want to save, like a straight red oak. Then I judge those beside it, figure out which trees crowd or compete for sunshine. Cutting these weaker, competing trees takes skill and practice, and I've had my share of trees hung up in the tops of others. But I've learned much about chain saws, wedges, and directional felling. If you want to practice TSI, spend time learning safe felling techniques.

According to Anderson, the best age to "release" a tree (i.e., cut the weaker neighbors to let in the sun) is ten to twenty years of age. This gives it twenty to thirty years to benefit from the additional light and nutrients before harvesting, if you plan to harvest. But Anderson also comments that most people don't cut enough, and this I can verify. Stands of young white pine that I did TSI to a few years ago are already crowded together again, and a few of the trees I left on the ice-damaged hillside are ill-formed and unhealthy. Though undamaged by ice, they too need to come out to make room for the pine and poplar saplings pushing up from the fertile ground.

That power, that rejuvenating energy, is one of the most remarkable aspects of a forest, that and its tremen-

dous beauty. By practicing TSI, I take part in this rejuve-
nation, and hopefully, also in the beauty. When we walk
in that forest today, the broken shelter has disappeared,
replaced by a green space of oaks and poplars healthy
and beautiful at last.

Green Lumber, Green Profits: Sustainable Forestry in Appalachia

Towns like to proclaim their history on those silver-colored, metal signs that greet every person coming into the burg. Williamsport, Pennsylvania, is no exception. I traveled Route 15 past the home of the Little League World Series and into the small city all four years of my undergraduate education. Every time I neared the city limits, I read the placard proclaiming Williamsport was once the Lumber Capital of the World, milling 350 million board feet per day during its peak, the highest level of lumber production on the globe. "Once" is the key word here. In the library, I found old photos of the timber boom, witnessed the broad West Branch of the Susquehanna jammed with logs, saw the loggers with their peaveys and axes, suspended pants, confident glare. In the background of every photo, the mountains lay naked. The boom didn't last but forty years.

That was in the mid-to-late 1800s, and the same type of timbering practices happened all over Appalachia. We were a growing nation hungry for wood. We still are. Now, over a hundred years later, our forests have started to mature again, and another timber boom is affecting our region. But other forms of logging are also taking shape, as more and more people see the need to avoid pine plantations and denuded mountains, and instead practice sustainable forestry.

But what does this buzzword "sustainable" mean when applied to our woods? Like the word "natural" in our grocery stores, the use of "sustainable" by different groups has slowly rendered it less and less specific. The industry's lead trade organization, the American Forest and Paper Association, accounts for 80 percent of wood products made in the United States and has pushed its "Sustainable Forestry Initiative" (SFI) program for the past few years. On the surface this program looks good. The Spring 2001 *Virginia Forest Landowner Update* newsletter, published by the Cooperative Extension at Virginia Tech, outlines SFI's mission and objectives. As the editor, Dylan Jenkins, writes, "The SFI Standard embodies a set of forest management practices that are economically and environmentally responsible and that maintain and improve long-term forest health and productivity." Their eleven objectives outline the specifics of this mission, from reforestation and water quality to education and outreach. In its brief history, the SFI program has accomplished much with many companies, like Westvaco, greatly improving their practices.

But as one logger told me, many believe SFI really just stands for "Same (Old) Forest Industry." Though SFI has encouraged companies to improve, one of the program's main purposes is to simply serve as a public relations vehicle. Michael Wagner writes in *The Amicus Journal* (from the Natural Resources Defense Council), "SFI doesn't tell companies what to do . . . It doesn't prescribe performance goals that [they] must meet in the field. Nor does it provide any enforcement." SFI Objective 5 illustrates the PR spin best: "Manage the visual impact of clear cutting and all other forest operations." The objective doesn't contend with the size or controversy of clear cuts, just "the visual impact." In other words, "sustainable" here applies to sustaining the company's image and dividends.

On the other end of the spectrum and on a much smaller scale, I found "sustainable" defined similarly by two different loggers in Southwest Virginia. My friend Harry Groot operates Next Generation Woods in Montgomery County, a small business that harvests, mills, and dries wood. In his business' newsletter, *Taking Root*, Groot defines sustainable as "the practice of forestry that results in a perpetually productive and balanced system." This "ecologically sustainable, economically sound, and socially responsible" system mimics nature by taking out the injured, crowded, diseased, and weak and leaving the strongest to continue growing.

Groot often uses the phrase "continuous canopy," harvesting trees in such a manner that the overall cover of leaves is only punctuated by very small openings of light. Contrast this continuous canopy with a clear cut, where most, if not all, of the trees are harvested. In the clear cut, little forest life survives to absorb eroding rains and dehydrating sun and wind. With a sustainably harvested forest, like Groot's eighty acres, as the worst trees are felled, the forest becomes healthier and more beautiful with each year. Harry Groot has been working his woods for eighteen years, even harvesting trees from one five-acre section twice in that time period. While the typical industry clear cut destroys the forest for a short-term gain, sustainable logging ensures a continuous supply of modest income and a healthy forest.

In Floyd County, Jason Rutledge, a horse logger—or, as he likes to call himself, a "biological woodsman"— agrees in principle with Groot, saying we should "take the worst first" whenever we harvest. At the 2001 Virginia Forest Watch Conference, though, Rutledge cautioned against using the term "sustainable" because he sees it as the industry's way of "bean counting," meaning that for every tree cut, you plant another. This is far from sustainable when you consider the overall health of our forests. From the hemlock woolly adelgid, chestnut blight, and gypsy moths, to strip mining, acid rain, cancerous sprawl, and a century of poor logging practices, our mountains are in a precarious condition. As Rutledge points out, "Our forests are declining, and you can't sustain a decline."

Instead of "sustainable," Rutledge uses the term "restorative forestry," a system which tries to manage forests to imitate pre-European contact. This method, like Groot's, focuses on selective cutting of individual trees, soil conservation using low-impact skidding methods (horses), and maintaining the diversity and health of all fauna and flora in the woods. As Groot argues, "This means never allowing high-grading," the conventional logging practice of taking only trees above a certain diameter. This practice "removes the most competitive trees and leaves the most genetically inferior to become the new forest. This is about as unnatural as possible."

One other critical distinguishing factor between conventional and sustainable loggers is the use of clear cuts. Groot writes that "clear cuts . . . should be a *rarely* used management tool because there's rarely a large natural opening in the canopy . . . [except for] smaller openings caused by an ice storm, wind, or disease." Rutledge agrees. They both contend that if the health of a particular stand is so poor from previous harvest practices, then small clear cuts up to two acres might be advisable. Compare this with the current industry's SFI limits. According to an article by Will Nixon in *American Forests*, "Companies must now limit these [clear] cuts to 120 acres, a dramatic drop from the 250- to 300-acre clear cuts" once implemented. Any plane ride over our mountains reveals acres upon acres of naked, eroding slopes. A two-acre clear cut would hardly be noticed.

Groot and Rutledge are not alone in their vision of a better way of harvesting timber. Their efforts are echoed internationally in the work of the Forest Stewardship Council (FSC), a non-profit, non-governmental organization founded in 1993. FSC's goal is to promote " . . . environmentally appropriate, socially beneficial and economically viable management . . . " of forest resources through the development of regional standards throughout the world.

Besides being much more stringent in their protection of the fragile ecology of the forest, FSC differs from the industry's SFI program by requiring third-party certification. The two current certifying organizations, Smart

Wood and Scientific Certification Systems, inspect a particular landowner's forest, verify for the public that the logger is meeting the FSC standards for selective cutting, and also provide a paper trail—or "chain of custody"—to follow each log as it gets milled and made into a final product. Much like the organic food program, these certifiers verify for the public that the wood has been harvested in a sound manner. In this way, FSC works for sustainable management of the whole system, from forest to finished product.

Another organization spearheading sustainable forestry is the Appalachian Sustainable Development (ASD) Forestry Program, based in the Clinch-Powell Watershed of Virginia and Tennessee. This program's two goals are to improve the quality of the region's forest practices and encourage local processing of forest resources. Adding value to the timber, through milling, drying, and planing, creates jobs and, in turn, boosts the local economy.

At a recent conference, Dennis Desmond, the ASD's forester, reviewed what his organization had accomplished in sustainable forestry, including logger training, landowner and consumer education, and identification of local woodworkers and builders who might use their product. The most impressive accomplishment, though, is

ASD's processing center near Castlewood, Virginia. This features a band-saw mill; a lumber storage shed; and a kiln powered by solar energy and wood-waste, with an annual capacity of three hundred thousand board feet. According to Anthony Flaccavento, director of ASD, they've invested over $500,000 in setting this up, and in so doing, they hope to create "the foundation of an alternative economic development approach that might be called an infrastructure for sustainability." They want their project to be both "market-driven and market-shaping," and their business plan projects that the wood products initiative should soon be financially self-sufficient.

Despite this progress, much more needs to happen. Wagner points out in *The Amicus Journal*, "For the FSC approach to work, to protect consumers while protecting the forest, more demand is needed—and, simultaneously, more supply." The percentage of sustainably managed forests globally and regionally is depressingly small, probably less than 10 percent, and a search through the Certified Forest Products Council's Web page (http://www.certifiedwood.org) reveals that Appalachia and the South lag behind the rest of the country. Most of the current certified wood comes from the Midwest, Northwest, Canada, and California. The demand continues to grow, though, as Home Depot and other lumber companies scramble to offer green wood products. Their demand is actually driving the industry to change, and consumers need to continue to vote with their green-backs if they want green lumber.

Two initiatives now underway in Appalachia might offer more insight into how to best stimulate supply and demand for sustainable wood. Michael Best—director of the Sustainable Mountain Agriculture Center (SMAC) in Berea, Kentucky—is presently conducting a market study to help small lumber producers market timber directly to consumers. One of the SMAC's goals is to keep small farms viable by helping the farmers fully use their woodlots, and to this end, the Center owns a band-saw mill and solar kiln. To study the market, Best sent questionnaires to professional and hobbyist woodworkers, including members of the Southern Highland Craft Guild. He wants to evaluate the woodworkers' needs, buying practices, and current sources of lumber. Once Best analyzes this study, he plans to design and implement marketing strategies that will allow the Center to use its mill and kiln as a model for other farmers and woodlot owners.

Groot, too, is working to connect sellers and buyers of "green" lumber. In Virginia—in addition to cutting, milling, and drying wood sustainably—he is focusing his efforts on creating a cooperative, called the Blue Ridge

Forest Cooperative. By pooling the resources of their forests and processing machinery (mill, kilns, etc.), the Co-op allows shareholders, all with third-party-certified forests, better access to the "green" market.

The Co-op also ensures that these landowners gain as much value as possible from their timber. If a landowner were to follow the sustainable practice of taking the worst trees first and leaving the best, he or she would lose money in the conventional timber market. But by milling and drying the lumber, the Co-op increases the worth of the goods for each member. Similar organizations in the Midwest already prove that, even while working within the capitalist system, members who practice sustainable forestry, responsible addition of value, and equitable profit sharing can still make money.

Sustainable forestry is only feasible, though, if we all participate, consumer and woodlot owner, Westvaco and every small logger. "The U.S. consumes nearly 20% more wood than it produces each year," informs Carl Fiedler in a recent *BioScience* article. By importing so much wood, we often also export many ecological disasters. Through conservation and recycling, we could eliminate that deficit, and through consumer demand, the industry might realize "green" lumber also means green profits as well as healthy forests.

The industry, however, doesn't own the majority of the woods. We do. Steve Lindeman includes this suprising fact in his "Forest Management as a Part of a Land Conservation Strategy." He quotes Rick Hamilton, forestry extension leader at North Carolina State University, as saying, "At least two-thirds of [the Southeast] is forested, [and] 70% is owned by private owners." Additionally, he continues, "less than 12% of these [private] owners have a forest management plan for their property. These forests are capable of producing a rate of return of 14-20%" through sustainable practices. These numbers show both our vast potential wealth and the great need for education.

Recently I drove by a logging site near my house. An outfit of loggers, some of them my neighbors, had clear cut an adjoining tract the previous year, stripped it as clean as those Pennsylvania mountains from the 1800s. Now they set up to spend the summer denuding the opposite mountain. On one of the logging trucks, I saw a lone bumper sticker targeting a regional environmental group as "99% Fact Free." We have a long way to go.

Conventional loggers and environmentalists, all community members, can and must come to the same table of sustainable forestry. But we need to all sit at this table together, at the same time, or the very wood used to make it may no longer exist.

A Rising Tide Floats All Logs

The oldest continuously operated land and cattle ranch in the United States recently gained well-deserved recognition for practicing one of the newest concepts in logging.

Southwest Virginia's Stuart Land & Cattle Company (SLCC) was formed in 1776 and owns 17,500 acres of pasture and timberland. In the past, SLCC had utilized most of this acreage for grazing cattle and cutting timber. All that changed in 2002, however. Under a pilot project with The Nature Conservancy, SLCC set aside 5,750 acres to be managed under a program that, if successful, would sustain the forest, protect the environment, and allow the company to make money in the process.

The deal took three years of preparatory work. In that time, The Nature Conservancy created the Conservation Forestry Program (CFP), whose aim was to protect and sustainably harvest forestland owned by private landowners. Like certificates of deposit, owners gave their timber rights to the CFP and in exchange received a modest, regular financial return (usually 4 to 4.5 percent) based on the timber's appraised value. The CFP guaranteed a permanent, healthy, working forest that supplied wood for the public and a consistent, annual return for the landowner.

Stuart Land & Cattle Company—located in one of the world's most diverse watersheds, the Clinch River—was the first landowner to join the CFP. Zan Stuart, SLCC president, explained, "This is a mutually beneficial arrangement that allows us to retain ownership of the land while being guaranteed an annual income in perpetuity. At the same time, the Conservancy will manage the timberland in an environmentally sound manner."

Steve Lindeman, manager of the CFP, planned to start timbering in 2003, after preparing a comprehensive management plan for the property. Most of the initial harvesting would consist of improvement cuts on thirty- to forty-acre sections, with the long-term goal of managing for high-grade hardwood sawtimber, which would mean growing better trees and cutting less.

All sides hoped this project would succeed, because all understood the challenges our forests faced—and still do face today. According to the United States Forest Service, the current harvest rate of pine trees in the South dramatically exceeds their growth rate. The same holds true for hardwoods. Much of this timbered land is clear cut and converted to pine plantations, sterile monocultures that can have 90 percent less biodiversity than the original hardwood stands.

The immediate problem for sustainable logging, however, is marketing low-grade lumber. Most forests have been poorly managed for the last century, depleting the stock of healthy trees and leaving only those of poorer quality to sell. Any type of sustainable forestry must first correct the problems created by generations of abuse, and this takes time, since a good hardwood takes at least a hundred years to mature.

But as Lindeman noted, "A rising tide floats all logs." He saw the CFP working with other similar organizations "to show that there's a better, more thoughtful way of doing this." To this end, the CFP partnered with Appalachian Sustainable Development, a nonprofit organization working in ten counties of Virginia and Tennessee, which constructed a solar kiln to dry lumber. Together the two organizations provided a model of how sustainable forestry can transform a region landowner by landowner, tree by tree.

Update: As of 2005, the CFP continues to work successfully in the Clinch River Watershed. Over seventeen thousand acres have been put under easement through this program, protecting the land from development, while also ensuring sound, ecological forest management.

A Different Fire: The Southern Pine Beetle

A fire has blazed through our mountains the last few years. It still burns—not the quick-spark, sudden-flame, all-consuming heat, smoke, and final blackness of a usual fire, but flames nonetheless. The spark of this blaze comes in the form of pheromones, sex-scents wafting on airwaves. These embers ignite into millions of grubs and their flames of hunger. The result is not the typical blackness but instead a brown skeletal forest, acres of pine trees all dead.

This is the fire of the southern pine beetle, a small creature with a huge appetite. The bug's bite is so big that in the past three years, I've watched it consume hundreds of acres of pine trees in both Floyd and Wythe Counties in Virginia. Portions of Macks Mountain in Floyd, and Sand and Iron Mountains in Wythe, are now covered with brown, dead needles where once a green forest stood.

This beetle prefers conifers in the yellow or black pine families, which in Appalachia means mainly pitch, table-mountain, and Virginia pines. Occasionally it will attack white pines, but usually that tree's defenses overwhelm the beetles.

When I first noticed the brown patches of mountain side, I figured the attacker had come from afar, like the invasive hemlock woolly adelgid that traveled from Japan or China on nursery stock and is slowly wiping out our beloved hemlocks. For the southern pine beetle, though, the south has always been home. In fact, some of the earliest settlers, the Moravians in North Carolina, chronicled their discovery of the insect's decimation of large pine forests. In 1797 the settlers tried to cut and salvage logs to slow the spread of the beetle. We have been fighting this bug ever since.

In recent history, the southern pine beetle has become the most destructive forest pest in the south. Between 1960 and 1990, it caused an estimated $900 million of damage. Luckily for us in the mountains, it attacks trees of low economic value, but through the rest of its range south into Mexico, it destroys more valuable species, especially the loblolly. Few controls have been found other than salvage and buffer cuts around affected areas.

The insect's biology serves it well. Usually cold winters (with two straight weeks below freezing) and good rainy seasons will keep the beetles in check and the trees healthy. But if we have a string of mild winters, more insects survive, and if we have a drought, more trees become stressed. Then, roughly every seven to ten years, the beetles' population explodes. Females will find a weak pine, send out pheromones, and start laying eggs. If enough adult beetles attack a tree, they'll quickly kill it. Trees normally "pitch-out" pests by sending resin to drown the bugs and fill the holes. But when the beetles' numbers explode up to a thousand per tree, the pines cannot keep up and the sap runs dry. The insects also girdle the inner bark and introduce a fungus called blue stain, both adding to the conifer's likely death.

Signs of an attack include brown needles; "pitch tubes," which are small, popcorn-like masses of resin; and a sawdust frass lodged in the bark. The adult beetles, brownish-black and roughly the size of a grain of rice, burrow S-shaped tunnels underneath the bark, their egg-laying chambers.

According to Dennis Anderson, state forester for Floyd County, the best method of control is through prevention, which means maintaining a healthy stand of trees. Have a forester create a management plan for your whole forest and include regular thinning cuts to promote diversity of species and avoid overcrowded trees. A thick stand often becomes the hot spot of an attack because of the trees' lack of vigor. If the beetle does attack, harvest what you can and cut a fifty- to seventy-foot buffer around the affected areas. Like a fire break, this should prevent the beetles' flame from spreading.

Although humans have struggled with this insect for hundreds of years and we've researched its life patterns extensively, the southern pine beetle continues to damage thousands of acres. Like the blackened spires after a fire, the brown swaths of dead pines attest to a powerful burning. Yet always under the starkness of dead trees, new seedlings sprout and fireweed blooms.

If you would like to read more about this fascinating beetle, take a look at the Appendix beginning on page 267.

Bullish Invasives

$\mathbf{M}$y morning walks have taken on an extra purpose. I still call the dogs who bound out and return full of the news of their noses. I still greet the sun and wind and dew and mountains and all living things. But now, I also chop some of those living things, mainly thistle and tree of heaven.

These two plants, along with many others, are invasives, aliens, colonizers that blow in on the wind and take over the pasture or wood's edge, slowly crowding out the native flora. The thistle makes worthless pasture and hay, since the cattle won't touch it.

Where I can, I mow the bristly, six-foot, prickly spires with the Bush Hog, the tractor scribing ever-smaller circles on the high knoll or front field. But on the steep slopes or among the trees, the tractor won't go, and so I walk and hoe, knowing I'll never fully succeed in this task. But maybe a field at a time, over the years, the hoe will chop free the grass, and other native plants like milkweed and ironweed will replace the thistle as a favorite of the butterflies.

Hacking through the thistle patches also makes me think of my maternal grandfather who died when I was one. Mom has told me stories of how he too would go out into the pasture and hoe all day, but what he hoed was blue thistle, or viper's bugloss, a plant common here in our fields as well. Its bright flowers lack the bristly thorns of its neighbor bull and Canadian thistle, so I save my energy for the more prickly. The blue-flowered alien, though, makes me realize how many more invasive plants we have now than my grandfather did a hundred years ago. P. D. Strausbaugh and Earl Core noted in their *Flora of West Virginia* that this invasive weed had already colonized West Virginia farms in 1802.

The other major exotic weed on our farm, tree of heaven (or ailanthus), I'm more hopeful about controlling. This small tree from China has leaves similar in appearance to sumac, but when crushed, they smell like pungent peanut butter, so we often call it stink tree. On our land, ailanthus has settled onto only a small section, maybe a half acre total, and not the whole farm. But it pays the difference with persistence. The first year, I sawed the trees, mainly two large ones with a scattering of a few smaller ones. I thought that would take care of the matter. The next year, where only five trees once stood, now a whole forest of seedlings appeared. This tree sprouts from roots, eruptions of foul-smelling leaves. So the second year, I mowed them all with a scythe, twice during the summer. They still came back. Finally, this past summer, I used a Pulaski, a fire-fighting tool that combines a hoe with a small axe, the ideal grubbing instrument. At each small grove of seedlings, I chopped the green trunks, then hoed up the ground, uncovering roots which I cut and pulled. The task blistered and callused my office-soft hands, but I think the majority of these aliens have finally died.

In all the literature about controlling invasive plants, the common chorus reads, "persistence." These plants succeed so well that their eradication is seldom quick, hence the need for regular attention with a hoe of some sort.

The literature also teaches that we're surrounded by aliens. On our farm alone, I've begun counting—coltsfoot, knapweed, multiflora rose, yellow flag, cocklebur, teasel, Johnsongrass, white clover, and three different kinds of thistle. This doesn't include the starling and all the other flora and fauna that I don't yet know. As Sarah reminds me, "They're everywhere."

Because *we* are everywhere. On our land where we built a new road, the knapweed and thistle thrive. Where previous owners logged, the forest openings are bull's-eyes for tree of heaven and multiflora rose. On a friend's farm, the bittersweet drapes its beautiful, smothering berries over their woodlot, bittersweet probably from someone throwing out a floral bouquet. And along the interstate, the kudzu slithers almost as fast as the truckers.

Ironically, what we hate we carry with us.

My neighbor used to say he changed from raising cattle to growing strawberries because plants don't jump fences. He was wrong. The bull might jump more dramatically, but the bull *thistle* slips through with ease. And maybe with more destruction.

Eastern Hemlocks
Fade From Our Forests

Every morning I walk by a hemlock so tall it holds up the sky. Its roots dip into Lost Bent Creek, and its branches lend wind song to the cadence of water rolling over rock. Nearby stand two structures probably built in the 1920s, a wooden bridge and a horse barn, its roof sagging like a saddle.

I have a photo from the 1940s of this bridge, this tree, and a farm horse named Silver. The horse looks to the camera, white-streaked forehead bright in the sun. A thin tether ties the horse to the hemlock, and whoever tied this leather had to hug it around the tree. The trunk looks big enough to be hard to hug, even for a grown man.

When I hug this tree today, my finger tips never touch, never come close to each other. Instead each finger holds onto slivers of bark and the rough grain marks my cheek.

This great tree is dying.

Like most hemlocks in our region, its green-forever life is slowly fading, sucked dry by a foreign insect, the hemlock woolly adelgid. If you turn a hemlock branch over and look under the needles, you'll likely see small, white, cottony masses. Those are the eggs of the bug. Like aphids, the tiny creatures attack the whole tree, pierce its bark, and bleed it to death. If dying trees had voices, the hemlock's moan would last five years, sometimes eight. The bugs take their time in killing.

The adelgid historically was never part of Southern nature. It came from Japan on a shipment of nursery stock that landed at Richmond, Virginia, in 1951. Like the accidentally introduced chestnut blight that killed a fourth of all Appalachian trees in the early 1900s, the adelgid has no natural enemies on this continent. Like that blight, the adelgid will dramatically change the structure of our forests, wiping out not only hemlocks but the fungi and finches, ferns and fish that depend on the tree's constant shade.

The coolness of these glens also supports large populations of salamanders plus 120 species of moss. Warblers, thrushes, and over ninety species of other birds nest in hemlocks, and native brook trout rely on the tree's ability to cool mountain streams. Twenty years from now, with hemlocks gone and ravine microclimates heated up, small streams may simply dry up.

A half mile upstream from our home, three hemlocks stand already dead, the woodpeckers chipping holes into bare spires. A mile downstream, the creek flows through a grove of hemlocks we call the Deep Woods. That dark, cool shade has slowly evaporated.

The adelgid has spread widely, hitching rides on the wind and wings of migrating birds. It now covers the Appalachian Range from Virginia to New England, with small outbreaks occurring in the Great Smoky Mountains.

According to Elizabeth Hunter, in Shenandoah National Park, 95 percent of the hemlocks showed good health in 1989; by 1998, that number dropped to less than 5 percent.

Science gives some hope: After years of study, Connecticut entomologists have released from quarantine a minute Japanese ladybug that prefers adelgids to all other foods. Those ladybugs have since been released in hemlock groves on public lands from North Carolina to New England. Other so-called biocontrols are also being tested. But time, as always, is of the essence. Scientists predict the adelgid will infest the whole range of eastern hemlocks within twenty years, and if we can save this tree, we need to do so within the next ten.

The woolly adelgid epitomizes the larger problem of invasive pests, six hundred of which cause an estimated $137 billion in damage annually across the United States. From the nutria, a beaver-like mammal in Maryland, to the Formosan termite in New Orleans, exotic species plague the South. Fraser firs, oaks, elms, dogwoods, butternuts, and beeches are all being ravaged by invasives.

Solutions? Ask the government to fund more monitor-
ing, research, and preventative measures. Stop the
import of invasive species before they arrive on our
shores. (Ironically, the nursery industry still imports many
known pest plants.) Push Congress and the president to
define "value," not just in commercial economic terms,
but also in ecological and aesthetic terms for species like
the hemlock. The 2000 National Invasive Species Council
created by President Clinton issued a draft plan to combat the invasives problem, but to date, Congress has
appropriated scant funding to implement it.

On an individual level, homeowners can protect orna-
mental hemlock trees by spraying them with dormant oil
or by hiring an expert to inject a pesticide into the tree
and soil. You can help curb the spread of invasive plants,
which severely harm native plant populations, by not
buying known invasives; avoid plants like purple looses-
trife or Japanese barberry. Also, use less fossil fuel. The
air pollution caused by coal and oil only exacerbates the
problem. Pollution-weakened trees, much like a person
who smokes two packs a day, fall prey more easily to disease and invasive attack.

Last summer I visited my aunt in Massachusetts. There,
I sat under hemlocks in their fine fullness—their shade

dense and cool, a rainfall of green needles. No cottony
mass of adelgids had found their way to those groves, yet.

I had forgotten the brightness of their new growth,
the light green of my childhood, of mountain fishing with
Grandpa in streams kept cold by hemlock shade. That
green I wanted to hold forever.

As with the dying hemlock at home, I hug a few of
these healthy trees to measure girth, to feel the rough
bark, the solid swell of living wood. I also hold new
shoulder-high seedlings, touch their willowy growth.
Hemlocks can live for eight hundred years. I pray these
trees will.

Beyond Bare-Ground: Organic Christmas Trees in the South

Folks normally think about Christmas trees once a year, when they pick out their holiday centerpiece at the local tree lot. But some of us who live in Christmas-tree–growing country contemplate these green pyramids daily.

In my travels throughout the southern mountains, I regularly see row upon row of blue-green cones, many on steep land. Our altitude makes for prime growing, especially of the best-selling tree, the Fraser fir, so tree growers cover hillsides with thousands of them. North Carolina alone has twenty-five thousand acres in production, and Virginia is close behind. Our region's trees travel as far away as Boston, Chicago, and, surprisingly, all the way to the Caribbean.

As the North Carolina Christmas Tree Association points out, growing these trees does benefit the environment. For example, "every acre of Christmas trees . . . gives off enough oxygen to meet the needs of eighteen people." The association also explains that Christmas trees "stabilize soil [and] protect water supplies," if farmers implement proper conservation methods.

But many tree-farming practices degrade our environment and disrupt natural balances. The industry, for instance, has made a verb of the phrase "bare-ground." To kill all the competitive weeds, you "bare-ground" a field with herbicides before planting and keep it "clean" with additional sprays for the next three years. This promotes fast-growing, well-shaped trees, but it also kills the soil life, wipes out beneficial insects, and causes erosion. Trees like firs thrive in cool, covered ground. As organic-tree grower Tom Brobson articulates, "'Bare-ground' is about as far from the tree's natural environment as possible."

Sadly, the same approach is applied to harmful insects and fungi. One pesticide commonly used, Di-syston 15-G, is so dangerous that a minute amount can harm and even kill farmworkers who, for want of time, often do not wear protective clothing. To make matters worse, many pests have become resistant to these chemicals, so the more you spray, the more you *have to* spray.

A few Christmas tree growers, however, challenge these conventional practices. They grow quality trees without massive amounts of harmful chemicals. I recently talked with four, all experienced in both conventional and organic methods, and all committed to the long term since it takes a tree six to ten years to mature. These growers tire of seeing fields covered at spray time with, as one puts it, workers in "zoot suits and gas masks."

Of this group, Curtis Buchanan in Mitchell County, North Carolina, has become the first and only farmer to produce certified-organic Fraser firs in the nation. Having grown trees most of his fifty years, he decided to experiment in 1995 by planting a separate, certified field. He wanted to prove that organic practices can render a tree of equal quality; he is close to reaching his goal.

Mark Lackey is another North Carolina grower who has proven that organic practices yield beautiful trees. These methods can also produce a field of weeds. But like the other three growers, Lackey has learned that weeds create the beneficial habitat needed for a healthy system. Lackey and entomologist Richard McDonald used grant money to monitor the populations of insects in his four-acre field and discovered huge numbers of predators controlling the aphids and mites that damage trees. Lackey mows once a year, mainly to herd the predators into the trees and make them do their work.

Tom Brobson and David Brady, like Buchanan and Lackey, have become bug and weed experts in addition to tree farmers. When he started in this business, Brobson learned how to grow trees using conventional methods, and he heard several older farmers connect their health problems with the sprays they used in the field. He didn't want to repeat their mistakes, so he and Brady have committed to organic practices for the long term. They're in their thirteenth year of production and beginning to reap the rewards of their hard work.

On their Clover Hollow Farm in Giles County, Virginia, Brobson and Brady plant fifteen acres with six different varieties of Christmas trees. These Virginia farmers don't fertilize as much as the other two growers in North Carolina (who use a variety of organic composts and fertilizers), so it takes nine years instead of the usual seven to grow a mature tree. Also, Brobson and Brady have found their firs lack the high-density of needles typical to conventionally-grown trees. Yet their firs are beautiful, and, as Brobson states, "We're finding customers like the appearance," as well as the knowledge of how they grow.

The two have found other successes as well. For Swiss needle cast, a fungus that kills needles, they've discovered that industrial-strength hydrogen peroxide, an organic solution, works well. For red spider mites, they've released predatory insects and promoted certain weed species, like yarrow, because these plants provide food and habitat for the beneficials. All of these practices controlled the problems, and though the two farmers are not certified organic, their customers know their practices help create a balanced system.

For marketing, Brobson and Brady rely on their computer. Both of the North Carolina farmers primarily move trees through wholesalers, but the Virginia growers sell directly to the customer. They've developed a network of churches and civic organization in the Washington, D.C., area where they sell 90 percent of their trees. The other 10 percent they sell to "choose-and-cut" customers who visit their farm on weekends. Because of their successful marketing, almost every tree is sold before it's cut, and Brady and Brobson struggle to meet the demand.

All four of these organic farmers also seek to make their farms sustainable through continual replanting, and Lackey has succeeded, growing his fourth rotation on the same land. Conventional farmers can't replant the same field because of massive amounts of pests, like the fungus phytothera root rot, "the cancer of the Christmas tree industry," according to Buchanan. Yet none of these organic farmers see it in their fields.

If more growers convert to these natural practices, and if more consumers demand organic trees, we might all help Lackey reach one of his goals. In a hundred years, he wants farmers to have to refer to old horticulture handbooks to remember the meaning of the verb "bare-ground."

Bowls for Christmas

For over forty years, Glendon Boyd has carved and sanded wooden bowls in his Floyd County shop, earning a living and carrying on a tradition by sculpting beautiful vessels of cherry, walnut, sassafras, cucumber, and many other woods.

We had seen Boyd at several craft fairs, and finally I asked him where he found his wood. He replied that he bought or traded for logs, and it became obvious that if we had quality wood, he'd willingly trade. We decided then to cut and barter our logs for these unique Boyd bowls to give to everyone on our Christmas list.

A massive cherry tree fallen across our stream became the first load, its red wood weighing down our truck. We traded and came home with a dough tray and several large, round bowls. We took another leaning cherry tree for the second load, and then two apple trees toppled by last winter's heavy snow became the third. The apple, he told us later, disappeared quickly at the craft shows.

The last load, sassafras, also helped our woods. I practiced timber stand improvement by cutting these four twisted sassafras trees that crowded pines and oaks that we wanted to grow more quickly. I felled the sweet-smelling sassafras, cut them into logs, and hauled them to Boyd on the day after Thanksgiving, in time to finish our Christmas shopping.

During this last visit, I asked him more specifically about how he created these wooden pieces. He started the traditional way his father taught him, "digging" out each bowl with a hand adze. Soon, though, to earn a living and meet the demand, he converted to using power tools. He first uses a chain saw to cut the logs into blocks and to rough out each bowl's shape. He never uses a lathe, but he does use other power tools to shape the platters, plates, trays, and bowls, making sure they have flat bottoms to prevent the wood from splitting. Boyd then lets the wood dry for six to eight weeks before he sands it three different times, and finally he coats each with cooking oil to prevent drying.

A true artist, Boyd whittles and creates other wooden beauties. One corner of his shop had several traditional wooden rakes, complete with a sapling split for a handle. Another corner had photos of his whittling masterpieces. His most elaborate and impressive artwork took roughly two years to finish "in his off hours." A small platform of gun-toting men, it depicts the famous Allen shoot-out in the Hillsville courthouse. The Blue Ridge Institute at

Ferrum College honored Boyd by displaying it recently in an exhibit of carved art.

Boyd is the fourth generation of his family to work with wood. His son, who also carves and helps sand the many bowls, has become the fifth, carrying on this tradition of turning a chunk of wood into a beautiful, useable bowl.

Handmade

Several years ago, Sarah began her first quilt, a nine-patch design, in early February. She cut and stitched the top, laid it out and pinned the three layers, and then, on her grandmother's frame, quilted the whole together. She labored over this through the winter, had to put it up for the summer berry season, and pulled it back out in the fall, working over it for hours every evening. With each tug of thread and needle, she stitched her love in this simple yet elegant blanket. I watched her through the whole process, yet she completely surprised me at Christmas when she gave me this beautiful, blue quilt. I hadn't realized she had labored so long to give the quilt as a gift.

We sleep under it now every night through the winter.

Before she died, another Sarah Minick, my grand-mother, labored over another quilt, a log-cabin pattern. From one of my shirts that no longer fit, she cut the red sparks in each square. I can trace other pieces of cloth to dresses she wore and shirts from my grandfather. She quilted crazily that year, because she gave each of her six grandchildren a quilt for Christmas, a piece of her heart that has already outlived her by decades.

When I look around our house, the list of gifts grows long: handmade birdhouses from my father-in-law; English walnuts, grown and cracked by my father; several needlepoint pillows and pictures from my mother-in-law; a cross-stitched wedding gift from my mother, the only one she ever tried; a writing desk like Thoreau's, built by my brother-in-law; a calligraphy of a favorite quote, done by my sister; and a wooden jigsaw puzzle of all the counties in Virginia, crafted by my uncle. All of these gifts are handmade, heart-made, beyond the value of a dollar.

Sarah and I try to do the same, giving homemade gifts instead of store-bought, especially during the holiday season. One fall we coiled and covered rope into beautiful, sturdy baskets. Sarah often knits caps and sweaters for others, including our dog. Lately she's created baskets—labor-intensive yet extremely beautiful works of art. From the garden, we've grown birdhouse gourds and fashioned them for wrens and bluebirds, and luffa gourds that became sponges given with handmade soap. Writing itself can be a gift. For one anniversary, we wrote for each other humorous short stories that recounted the past year, like the time I cut a walnut tree that fell, not away from the house, but onto it.

Meaningful gift-giving is never as simple as opening the wallet. Our money has little to show it belonged to us, its value rendered by other people, not the gift-giver or receiver. I'm thankful when I receive money as a gift, but in a year's time, I can never remember the money or the giver or what I bought.

We're getting ready for this Christmas. In our kitchen pantry, a whole shelf gleams with pint-sized purple jewels, blueberry jam Sarah put up this summer. She made extra to celebrate the harvest of our blueberry business. And to share in this celebration and the joy of the season, all of our relatives will receive blueberry jam—homemade, of course.

Following Myself Home

Night Walking

The moonlight slowly washes down our small valley, tree limb by tree limb, pushing out the darkness. In the deep woods behind the berry field, I hear the male great horned owl and then the female's quick reply. The night is the owl's domain, and I am only a brief visitor.

In the winter, when I arrive home from work, the night has already come. But our dogs, Little B and Becca, still expect their evening jaunt with or without daylight, and after sitting all day in an office, my body also asks for a hike. So while the dogs impatiently prance and play, I change clothes, grab a flashlight, and head out, hoping to be as alert to the new night's smells and sounds as the tail-wagging pair in front of me.

I stick to paths I know, like our farm road to the pond, the bumps and potholes familiar, the track clear of roots and limbs. Caught up in the dogs' excitement, I go fast and find myself huffing at the top of the hill. It is always this way, and always, when I catch my breath, I blow away the day's tension and proceed more slowly. It takes that initial rush, it seems, to get me out of my head full of tasks and worries, and focused on the place where I walk.

Tonight the sky is clear, the snowpack bright, the walking easy in the light of the almost-full moon. To the east, his star-studded belt shows Orion has risen again, and above him, I see the small cluster of stars known as the Seven Sisters. The moon is too bright this time to see all seven, but occasionally, I can see them all holding close together. They make me think of the Kiowa story, told by Joseph Bruchac, of how the sisters escaped a bear by becoming stars.

I walk on my shadow, the moonlight casting it ahead onto the snow, and because of all the brightness, I don't use the flashlight at all. But even on cloudy, moonless nights, I rarely use the light. I've learned to trust my night vision more and more. This peripheral vision is dominated by rods, the cells in our eyes sensitive to light and motion, as opposed to the cones, which pick out color. At night the cones are fairly useless, and the more a person can adapt to using peripheral vision, the better one can see. Some equate this ability to having "second vision," or the ability to see more than just the surface. I haven't found this "second vision" yet, but I do value and enjoy getting out at night and seeing the world in a different way.

I'm not alone. A friend gave me an old article written by Nelson Zink and Stephen Parks called "Nightwalking," and in it, the authors explain both how to night walk and why. One of the tricks is to develop and eventually trust your peripheral vision. You do this by *not* looking directly at what you want to see. Focus instead on a point about twelve inches from the tip of your nose. They suggest attaching a short stick to a baseball cap so that its tip is directly in line with your nose at eye level. Focus on this tip as you walk. With or without this modified ball cap, practice night walking on familiar paths and in safe places. Take a friend and pick a night with little or no moon and a place with no artificial light. Ironically, too much light makes peripheral vision difficult and even painful.

Give yourself time. Zink and Parks explain that it takes the rods in our eyes thirty minutes to fully adjust to the darkness. It also takes practice and several hours of walking to fully develop this peripheral vision. The trick is to "look around" by moving your attention but *not* your eyes, to become aware of what surrounds you by using peripheral vision.

Though I haven't yet fully experienced this "second vision," I do know that I am much more relaxed after my nightly sojourns. The dogs and I pause by the frozen pond, then turn to head home, the hoot owl giving a benediction to our night walk.

Following Myself Home

The new snow delivers the night's news.

Yearling deer scampered through our cornfield, scattering kernels. Heart-shaped prints run in circles of play.

Near our house, larger prints end and begin on opposite sides of the garden fence; scruffed-up snow reveals nibbled grass.

Upstream on a well-traveled path that crosses the creek, hoofprints jump from bank to ice and, surprised, slide three feet. I can almost hear the snort and clatter.

The ghosts of deer are not all I see. In the raspberry patch, a possum's tail wiggles between its paw prints, a long line dotted on both sides, like the shadow of a giant centipede. I imagine the possum's low grunts as it roots for seed or grubs.

Nearby I find the wing prints of a chickadee. The tiny bird bent over the dried flower head of a Queen Anne's lace, ate the seeds, and flew off. Each feather tip marked the snow, finer than any angel's wings.

From tree to tree, squirrel tracks scamper, front paws together, back paws apart, running like a rabbit. Does the squirrel remember enough to find the nuts she buried months ago? One gray squirrel scolds me from her perch high in an oak, then jumps to another oak and squeezes into a small hole, her bushy tail flapping all the way.

Up our spring hollow, turkey tracks lead me everywhere, through the stream, under the spicebush, up and down several banks. Then all these three-toed, backward-pointing arrows congregate at a fallen, wild grapevine. They trample the whole area, as if at a dance, scratching to summer's old music of seeds and dried fruit.

In the blueberry field, I find clumps of feathers scattered among several bushes, but no tracks. The feathers I can't identify, maybe a sparrow, but the lack of tracks puzzles me more. What creature killed and ate this small bird without leaving a trace except these feathers? A fox or weasel I could follow to their dens. An owl would have killed with its talons and carried it back to its nest of young, leaving no remains. Maybe a hawk, a sharp-shinned, bulleted through these bushes, caught the surprised little bird, and left some feathers as it flew off. I can't figure it out, and wander on with a clump of the speckled feathers in my pocket.

At the pond, I walk on water and find I'm not the first to do so. In the night, the raccoon that lives in the hollow gum waddled across this ice, taking the shortcut to the woods beyond. What did his callused paws feel of this rough ice, and how did he know to trust it? What faith does he know?

I follow the raccoon's prints past the maze of uprooted hemlocks. Years ago, under one of these fallen trees, I traced the path of a bobcat who sought shelter from a blizzard. I had never seen the big cat's prints before, as delicately placed as any house cat. In its temporary den, protected from the storm, it scratched and circled the ground, then curled up to sleep and wait. I touched the bobcat's bed, my hand seeking any remaining warmth.

This new sheet of white reveals no bobcat den, no scribble of tracks, just the cup of an oak leaf filled with white fluff. I turn then, my boots finding their own just-made path, and footprint by footprint, I follow myself home.

Appendix

Publications and Resources

Floating

To Pond

Publications

Tim Matson, *Earth Ponds Sourcebook: Pond Owner's Manual and Resource Guide* (Woodstock, VT: Countryman Press, 2004).

—, *Earth Ponds: The Country Pond Maker's Guide* (Woodstock, VT: Countryman Press, 1988).

The Return of the Beaver

Publications

Donald Linzey, *The Mammals of Virginia* (Blacksburg, VA: McDonald and Woodward Publishing, 1998).

Hope Ryden, *Lily Pond: Four Years with a Family of Beavers* (Guilford, CT: Globe Pequot Press, 1997).

Dorothy Richards. *Beaversprite: My Years Building an Animal Sanctuary* (Interlaken, NY: Heart of the Lakes Publishing, 1984).

Sea Turtles

Publications

Jeff Ripple, *Sea Turtles* (Stillwater, MN: Voyager Press, 1996).

Resources

Many folks vacation at the beach. Wherever that beach is, a sea turtle probably tries to nest on the dunes. Here are a few rules to ensure the turtle nests successfully:

- Don't touch or disturb turtles crawling to or from the ocean, and give them space to move freely.

- Don't shine lights in their eyes or use flash photography.

- If you are in a beach house, turn off the outside lights in May through September. Lights disorient the turtles, causing them to wander inland rather than toward the sea.

- Avoid driving on the beach as the ruts from tire tracks can trap hatchlings. Report nests, hatchlings, or sick or injured turtles.

- Put a cage on any recreational-boat propeller.

- Avoid polluting, wherever you are. Sea creatures often choke and die from eating balloons or plastic grocery bags, mistaking them for jellyfish. As Jean Beasley said, "We will never stop the deaths of these creatures, but we can surely do a better job of living with them."

- Tell others, including your elected officials.

- Donate to the sea turtle hospital (PO Box 3012, 822 Carolina Blvd., Topsail Beach, NC 28445). They are vastly overcrowded and planning to build a new facility. Plus, five thousand pounds of squid a year isn't cheap.

- You can visit the hospital during the summer, beginning in June. It is open from 2:00-4:00 p.m. every day except Sundays and Wednesdays, and it is a working hospital, so emergency closings sometimes occur. You can visit their Web site any time of year at http://www.seaturtlehospital.org.

Flying

Nests

Publications

Paul Ehrlich, David Dobkin, and Darryl Wheye, *The Birder's Handbook* (New York: Simon and Schuster, 1988).

Vanishing Birds

Publications

Carol Kaesuk Yoon, "More Than Decoration, Songbirds Are Essential to Forests' Health," *New York Times,* 8 Nov. 1994, B11, C4.

Monarchs: Flying Poetry

Publications

Pat Durkin, "Migrating Monarch Butterfly," *National Geographic News,* 22 Nov. 2000. http://news.nationalgeographic.com/news/2000/11/1122_monarchs.html

Resources

Ways to ensure this winged royalty's health include avoiding herbicides and pesticides, creating butterfly gardens, or even allowing certain weeds to bloom. Or you can join the thousands of other butterfly lovers and monitor monarchs' migrations. Teachers, students, families, and individuals all across the continent tag butterflies and then communicate with each other to follow the flying miracles' yearly movements. For more information, visit Monarch Watch on the Web at http://www.monarchwatch.org.

Homes for the Holidays

Resources

For more specific information on bats and bat houses, contact Bat Conservation International, PO Box 162603, Austin, TX 78716; or the American Bat

Conservation Society, P O Box 1393, Rockville,
MD 20849.

Gathering

Have Fungi, But Be Careful

Publications

Jennifer Snyder, *The Shiitake Way: Vegetarian
Cooking with Shiitake Mushrooms* (Summertown,
TN: Book Publishing, 1993).

Resources

Sources for mushrooms and spawn:

Often at farmers' markets, you can find individuals
who grow and sell shiitake mushrooms and logs, so
check your local market for a fresh supply. If you
want to buy spawn to inoculate your own logs, two
sources I've worked with are: Mushroompeople,
P O Box 220, Summertown, TN 38482-0220,
(615) 964-2200; and Hardscrabble Enterprises, Inc.,
P O Box 1124, Franklin, WV 26807, (304) 358-2921.

Preparation of Shiitake:

I like to just sauté mushrooms in butter and eat them
as a side dish, but this recipe tastes great as well:

"Shiitake Stroganoff"
from Jennifer Snyder, *The Shiitake Way*

Ingredients for 4 servings: 1½ cups non-fat yogurt;
1 t. Dijon mustard; 1½ T. olive oil; 2 med. onions, thin-
ly sliced; 4 cloves garlic, minced; 1½ pounds fresh shiitake (4 C.), stems removed, sliced; ⅓ cup apple cider
vinegar; salt and pepper to taste; paprika.

Mix the yogurt and mustard, and set aside.

In a large sauté pan, heat the oil over medium-high
heat. Add onions and cook until softened. Reduce
heat to low and add garlic and mushrooms. Cook

10 minutes, stirring constantly. Add vinegar, and cook 10-15 minutes, until mushrooms are tender. Remove from heat and stir in yogurt. Season with salt and pepper, and sprinkle with paprika. Delicious over baked potatoes, rice, or noodles.

Growing Ginseng

Publications

Two sources for information to get started: Scott Persons' *American Ginseng: Green Gold* (Asheville, NC: Bright Mountain Books, 1986) covers just about everything you need to know about this crop, from how to grow it to how to take it medicinally. Andy Hankins, the Virginia Extension specialist for alternative agriculture, also has a wealth of information from his experiments growing wild simulated ginseng for the last decade. His paper, "Producing and Marketing Wild Simulated Ginseng in Forest and Agroforestry Systems," is available at the Virginia Tech Non-timber Forest Products Web site at http://www.sfp.forprod.vt.edu or you can contact Tom Hammett at (540) 231-2716 for a copy.

Resources

Two other sources for buyers and growers: North Carolina Natural Products Association, and United Plant Savers, a non-profit education corporation dedicated to preserving native medicinal plants. They can be reached at http://www .ncnaturalproducts.org and http://www .unitedplantsavers.org, respectively.

For advice on soil tests, contact your local county extension office.

A "Woods Garden" Full of Cohosh

Publications

Richo Cech, *Growing At-Risk Medicinal Herbs* (Williams, OR: Horizon Herbs, 2002).

Steven Foster and James A. Duke, *The Peterson Field Guide to Medicinal Plants* (Boston: Houghton Mifflin, 1990).

Resources

If you want to grow woodland herbs in your own woodlot, consider first joining United Plant Savers. They also publish an excellent newsletter, and their Web page (http://www.unitedplantsavers.org) includes a list of nurseries that ethically propagate medicinal herbs.

One other organization with similar goals is The National Center for Preservation of Medicinal Herbs. Their Web site is located at http://home .frognet.net/~rural8/frames2.html. Both sites offer links as well as advice on how to grow these plants.

In Praise of Pawpaws

Resources

The Pawpaw Foundation, 147 Atwood Research Facility, Kentucky State University, Frankfort, KY 40601. They'll send you information on nurseries, pawpaw production, recipes, and a regular newsletter. You can also visit the Web site at http://www .pawpaw.kysu.edu.

Growing

Grow a Patch of Your Own *and* Shocked

Resources

For more specific information on strawberries and deer fencing as well as a wide variety of agricultural topics, contact: Appropriate Technology Transfer for Rural Areas (ATTRA), PO Box 3657, Fayetteville, AR 72702, (800) 346-9140, or on the Web at http://www.attra.ncat.org.

Gray Buffalo

Publications

Gretel Ehrlich, *A Match to the Heart* (New York: Penguin, 1994).

Health, Hunger, and Hunting

Publications

Richard Nelson, *Heart and Blood: Living With Deer in North America* (New York: Knopf, 1997).

We Create the World We Eat:
The Benefits of Organic Food

Publications

Eric Schlosser, *Fast Food Nation: The Dark Side of the All-American Meal* (New York: Perennial, 2002).

Bob L. Smith, "Organic Foods vs. Supermarket Foods: Element Levels," *Journal of Applied Nutrition* 45, no. 1 (1993): 35-9.

Virginia Worthington, "Nutritional Quality of Organic Versus Conventional Fruits, Vegetables, and Grains," *The Journal of Alternative and Complementary Medicine* 7, no. 2 (2001): 161-173 (accessed on the Organic Trade Association's Web page, http://www.ota.com, 9 March 2003).

Rob Edwards, "The Natural Choice: Organic Food Has More of What It Takes to Keep You Healthy," *New Scientist* 73 (16 March 2002).

Cynthia Curl, Richard Fenske, Kai Elgethun, "Organophosphorus Pesticide Exposure of Urban and Suburban Preschool Children with Organic and Conventional Diets," *Environmental Health Perspectives* 111, no. 3 (March 2003).

Barbara Kingsolver, *Small Wonders* (Waterville, ME: Thorndike, 2002), 188.

Beyond Organic

Publications

Joan Dye Gussow, *This Organic Life* (White River Junction, VT: Chelsea Green, 2001).

Resources

Visit http://www.localharvest.org, a Web site dedicated to connecting farmers directly with consumers.

Star Linked

Publications

Rachel Massey, "Biotech Basics: A Four-Part Article," *Rachel's Environment and Health News* 716 (17 Jan. 2001). You can find more useful information at http://www.organicconsumers.org.

Michael Hansen, "Starlink Corn and Food Allergies—Dr. Michael Hansen's Testimony to the EPA," EPA Docket Number OPP-00688, 28 Nov. 2000.

Sally Deneen, "Food Fight: Genetic Engineering vs. Organics: The Good, the Bad and the Ugly," *E: The Environmental Magazine* (July/August 2003).

Not Ready for Roundup's Results

Publications

Lennart Hardell and Mikael Eriksson, "A Case-Control Study of Non-Hodgkin Lymphoma and Exposure to Pesticides," *Journal of the American Cancer Society* 85, no. 6 (1999): 1353-60.

Caroline Cox, "Glyphosate (Roundup): Herbicide Factsheet," *Journal of Pesticide* Reform 18, no. 3 (Fall 1998): 3-17.

David Barboza, "The Power of Roundup: A Weed Killer Is a Block For Monsanto To Build On," *New York Times*, 2 Aug. 2001. http://www .organicconsumers.org/monsanto/booming080601 .cfm (accessed 30 Jan. 2003).

You can find out more about leukemia and lymphoma at http://www.llcare.org.

The Trouble with "Waste"

Publications

Wendell Berry, *The Unsettling of America* (San Francisco: Sierra Club, 1996).

Working Among Trees

Green Lumber, Green Profits: Sustainable Forestry in Appalachia

Publications

Dylan Jenkins, "Five Years of the Sustainable Forestry Initiative in Virginia," *Virginia Forest Landowner Update* 15, no. 2 (Spring 2001): 1, 5-6. (Contact at 238 Cheatham Hall [0324], Blacksburg, VA 24061.)

Michael Wagner, "Building Forests, Growing Homes," *The Amicus Journal* 19, no. 1 (Spring 1997).

Harry Groot, "Why Sustainable Forestry?" *Taking Root* 1, no. 1 (Spring 2001): 1, 3-4. (Contact at Next Generation Woods, Inc., 4615 Mountain Pride Rd., Hiwassee, VA 24347.)

Will Nixon, "Can We Make Our Forests Last?" *American Forests* 101, no. 5-6 (May-June 1995): 14-18.

Anthony Flaccavento, "Building an Ecobusiness Infrastructure in Appalachia," *In Business* magazine 21, no. 5 (Sept./Oct. 1999): 19-21.

Carl Fiedler, Stephen Arno, Charles Keegan, Keith Blatner, "Overcoming America's Wood Deficit: An Overlooked Option," *BioScience* 51, no. 1 (Jan. 2001): 53-58.

Steve Lindeman, "Forest Management as a Part of a Land Conservation Strategy: A Report on a Recent Workshop Held in Sanford, NC on February 22-23, 2001," *Under the Canopy: Newsletter of the Southeast Region of Forest Stewards Guild,* no. 2 (Spring 2001): 4-6.

A Rising Tide Floats All Logs

Publications

Andrew George, "Don't Be Fooled—Pine Plantations Are Not Forests," *Asheville Citizen-Times,* 9 April 2002.

A Different Fire: The Southern Pine Beetle

Publications

James Meeker, Wayne Dixon, and John Foltz, "The Southern Pine Beetle, *Dendroctus frontalis* Zimmerman," Florida Department of Agriculture and Consumer Services, Entomology Circular no. 369 (March/April 1995).

Eric Day, "Southern Pine Beetle Factsheet," Virginia Cooperative Extension, Entomology Publication 444-243 (1997).

The Bugwood Network-University of Georgia, "History of Southern Pine Beetle Control" (2002), http://www.barkbeetles.org/spb/HxofSPBC.html (accessed 2 Sept. 2002).

Bullish Invasives

Publications

P. D. Strausbaugh and Earl Core, *Flora of West Virginia*, 2nd ed. (Morgantown, WV: Seneca Books, 1964).

Eastern Hemlocks Fade From Our Forests

Publications

Elizabeth Hunter, "Will Hemlocks Go the Way of the Chestnut?" *Appalachian Voice*, July 2001.

Beyond Bare-Ground:
Organic Christmas Trees in the South

Resources

The North Carolina Christmas Tree Association's Web site can be accessed at http://www .ncchristmastrees.com.

Following Myself Home

Night Walking

Publications

Nelson Zink and Stephen Parks, "Nightwalking: Exploring the Dark with Peripheral Vision," *Whole Earth Review*, Fall 1991, 4-10.

Jim Minick lives, writes, and farms in southwest Virginia, while also teaching writing and literature at Radford University. His poems and essays have appeared in many books and periodicals including *Orion, Shenandoah, YES!, Natural Home, Encyclopedia of Appalachia, Appalachian Journal, Appalachian Heritage,* and *Wind.* Since 1996, Minick has written a regular column for the "New River Valley Current" section of *The Roanoke Times,* as well as other articles that have appeared in major newspapers throughout the South.